Imagination's Many Rooms

Amatoritsero Ede

Griots Lounge Publishing
Canada

Published in 2022 by
Griots Lounge Publishing Canada
www.griotslounge.ca
Email: info@griotslounge.ca

IMAGINATIONS MANY ROOMS
Copyright © 2022 Amatoritsero Ede

Library and Archives Canada Cataloguing in Publication

ISBN: 978-1-7776884-9-3

Cover Art by Gabriel Ogungbade
Interior Design by Rachelle Painchaud-Nash

Printed and bound in Canada

Reminiscences

AKÉ

The Years of Childhood

WOLE SOYINKA

*For Godwin Ede,
with sincere wishes
for a successful
writing career.*

[signature] June 82

REX COLLINGS   LONDON   1981

4

Going to Meet 'The Man'

A dazed eighteen-year-old (obsessed with writing and armed with a notebook of juvenile poems) struck out in the direction of Ife to seek validation from one of the most visible literary minds of his country. It was June of 1982, the dying days of a rogue regime, which had forced a decade-old oil-boom economy unto its knees. Two regimes later, it would get a death-shove with the infamous 'Structural Adjustment Program.'

Fresh out of high school and full of hope and vague intimations of where life was supposed to be heading in a spiritually and economically depressed social space, one fed less on food than on dry paper—doses of cheap literature at first; Donatus-Nwoga-edited *West African Verse*; medieval English masterpieces by Geoffrey Chaucer; John Dryden; Alexander Pope; the English Romantics and an early-modernist Gerald Manley Hopkins, who yammered on about 'inscape' and 'instress.' In the country's prevailing economic and political hopelessness, his lean hungry frame sought spiritual succour in the dusty old city of Ife, where The Man was culture's 'high priest'—he was known to produce his plays there; he was a lecturer at the university there. From his seat at Ife, he obsessed his country's literary imagination, and the imagination of this young nobody seeking him out.

Money for the journey had been somehow purloined from a long-suffering grandmother in Oke-Odo, Ibadan. And then off to the motor park somewhere on old-Ife Road. The ride was smooth; the plan as vague as the premonition of doom engendered by a rotten body politic. There was this schooled but uneducated primary school teacher posing as President. In his startled, spherical eye-glasses he looked as unfit for the highest office in the country as a schoolboy in a Vice-Chancellor's chair. How did it come about that an impostor such as Shehu Shagari was President in a country with heads as round as that of a Wole Soyinka or a Tai Solarin?

There was an arrangement to squat with a new acquaintance, a fellow dreamer and 'eccentric'—the opinion of his traditional environment—who read esoteric literature with titles such as *Fourteen Lessons in Yogi Philosophy and Oriental Occultism* or *Entering the Silence*, practiced Hatha Yoga, and had a Brown Belt in Blue Wave Karate. He had just relocated to Ife and worked in a super-market. Born as Ade Ifakolujo, he had, in a rebellious mood against a querulous Ekiti father, hyphenated his name to Ade Fakolujo-Spence! Where the 'Spence' came from was all conjecture. He was older and therefore 'brother Ade' in the usual traditional Yoruba way of showing deference to age. Arrival was expected. Getting to Ade's workplace from the motor park was not too difficult when one asked for directions. They left there together and headed for his house. He lived well, exercised well, ate well, was round- and oily-cheeked and admonished against smoking.

"How can you smoke and do breathing exercises after?"

One merely shrugged. Smoking was a way of telling a repressive adult world, "Go to hell!" He had his name-switch; one had one's John Players or Benson and Hedges. One young man's father was an ogre; the other's a monster, who was securely locked up in the past. There lay the connection, cigarette smoke or not, apart from a shared interest in the esoteric. The purpose of the journey was enough to exonerate. How in hell would The Man be reached? The nerve of it! He was exhilarated, too, and liked the idea that one wrote poetry of whatever quality.

The next day, all roads led to the University of Ife. It was a bit of a ride since the campus is on the outskirts, seats on the lip of the city, sort of tucks into itself like a shy guest at a meal. It was the retreat of high culture. The distance from the main gate, with its imposing arches, to the centre of campus was itself quite a stretch of tarmac. But the bus ride finally came to an end. The surrounding architecture was awe-inspiring. It was a relatively new university, built by Obafemi Awolowo from the sale of cocoa-produce money in the 1960s. It is remembered as a sprawling, giddy campus set down among undulating, hunch-backed grounds, with well-maintained roads and a rich faculty living quarters detached from the main campus by a network of freshly tarred roads glinting in the burning sun. The overall impression was that of looking down imperiously on the dusty grey city of Ife from any high point on that hilly campus. 'Great Ife!' indeed, as its students and alumni still refer to it. At least, that was the impression when one looked down from the corridors of the English Department, where The Man was known to lecture in Comparative Literature.

Enquiries had been made but he was nowhere to be found. He was known to have strange disappearing acts—either globe-trotting or going off on sudden bouts of game-hunting in the forest with one rumoured friend, Femi Johnson. So, the next thing to do was to go and try to locate his residence in the staff quarters, almost a quarter of a mile away from the centre of campus. It was a long, tiring walk on this veritable 'highway' within the self-enclosed campus town. Highway it was because one hardly met a soul. One would not want to traverse that stretch without a car. They roared by intermittently. Both sides of the road were wooded. Thumbing a ride was impolitic, so march, march! The mirage on the black snaking road made one dizzy. The sun was merciless in its ferocity that day. The road's throat was parched. One could have drunken of the dust on the

7

embankment, with its huge shoulders of earth and grass and wood and, of course, game. It was well-known that he loved to hide. Well, were writers not strange beings, making a spindly-legged youth have to walk all this way without guarantee of fulfilment at the end of the search?

Finally, a curve in the endless road revealed a house fitting the descriptions received earlier through discreet enquiries of strangers on campus and from the occasional ambler along the way. It stood alone on its own grounds, shunning the curiosity of neighbours. Predictably, it was securely locked, windows, door, and jamb shut-mouthed. A jeep was parked before the residence, a dust-caked tarpaulin thrown over it. Yes, it must have been the right house. He was known to love jeeps. They could rapidly gain the brush and brambles of hunting grounds in the woods. Perhaps he was abroad again. But it was said he was in town and had been seen yesterday. One made the long trek back to the campus; took a bus into the city and to Ade's, determined to make another foray the next day. It was said by the porters at the English Department that he might be in his office tomorrow.

The following day was more rewarding. At the porters' lodge there was no cooperation this time. Yes, he had been seen going up to his office, but no you cannot go up there. And, demurring, one turned away, melted into the next pillar around the corner, then surreptitiously made a quick dash from the other side of the porter's lodge into the stairway, crouched and bounded up like a cat. It was easy to find the well-known name on one of the doors along the corridors. It was a solid double-door. A plaque on it read, simply, "Wole Soyinka." A soft knock on the door and a mellifluous voice in a soft baritone urged, "Come in!"

Nervous at this planned but unbidden intrusion, one turned the doorknob, pushed gently, and stepped into a spacious office. The

Man raised his eyebrows in a slight surprise. There was a pause. Recovering from a complex of incredulity, shock, and excitement at the imposing presence leaning back into a black upholstered swing chair, the intruder quickly explained, "Please, sir, don't be annoyed with the porters; they did not let me through, but I sneaked up!" That was open sesame. Perhaps a cord was struck by such a singularly rebellious admission. One knew that he was a maverick himself. The ghost of a smile played on his face. "What can I do for you?" And disbelief as a hand waved one into the chair opposite his spacious but tidy desk. On the floor, to one side of the desk, was a tall carton full of new-minted books in hardcover. Now one remembered the old notebook of juvenilia and proffered it with, "I want you to see some of my poems." He smiled, reached out a hand and accepted the Magnum Opus! "I do not really make comments on other people's work. But I will look at it." He observed the tangle of fresh youth and inexperience before him.

"What are you doing now?"

"I just finished secondary school last year; I am trying to get into university."

"How old are you?"

"I am 18."

There was a pause. Something was wrong?

"You better buck up! Those young boys out on the campus are not much older than you. Some are even 16."

If only he knew what artificial obstacles stood in one's way; if only he knew that one fed only on hope every waking day under the terrible socio-economic and political dispensation of the day! But, for a boy who had been forced to kill his own father in his heart, there was the warm gratification that his was a fatherly rethought.

"Ehm...Could you come back tomorrow at about—."

9

A time was given and acknowledged. It was the first formal appointment.

"By then I will have looked at your poems."

The next day's meeting went without a hitch. The porters were cooperative. Up the stairs with more confidence, a timid knock, and the same voice as yesterday despite fears that The Man might not be there to receive an insignificant caller; the same mix of nervousness and exhilaration in the youth, who timidly asked, "How do you find the poems?"

The Man was ready. The notebook lay on the desk suggesting it had, at least, been reviewed. One was worried. The notebook contained such esoteric stuff in imitative scansion as, "That still moment of eternal bliss/One knows not what to call/Samadhi..." Some more original material like the idyllic "Bobbing Carpets of Blackness" on seeing birds fly across the sky in concert on one evening. Later on, more conscious imitations of medieval English scansion, "When Christ Lord did a promise make/Of life eternal to simple souls...," would follow.

"You know as I said, I never really make comments. But it's coming up; it's coming up! Have you been published before?"

"No!"

"Well, try the newspapers; join the Association of Nigerian Authors, try reading on the Radio."

The information was soaked up.

"Then when you have the psychological moment, you approach a publisher. The path is narrow and those who are called are few."

This biblical allusion was a bit ironic since The Man was known to be agnostic. And one had read the collection, *Idanre,* and the poem "Abiku"; both were rich in the mythopoetic and the animistic. But the advice was noted and diligently followed up on later. One's eyes lighted on the carton of new books beside the desk again.

"That's a new book?"

The man observed the youth, looked in the direction of interest.

"Yes.Itjustcameout."Andunexpectedly,"Wouldyoulikeacopy?"

"Yes, yes!"

He had already leaned forward in his swivel chair, bent down a bit, and swiftly procured a copy out of the carton. It was already open on his desk.

"What's your name?"

"Godwin Ede"

"How do you spell the last name?"

He scribbled into the prelims of the book and handed over this treasure. It was *Ake: The Years of Childhood.* The autograph read, "for Godwin Ede, with sincere wishes for a successful writing career." And the flourish of a signature! Then it was dated, "June 82." The book became a talisman and a constant reminder of the prognostications of the wishes of the autograph. One had to succeed as a writer, no matter what. It was also a challenge too, that autograph. The time came to leave.

"Eh…I do not have money for the journey back to Ibadan!"

The Man dipped into his pockets and proffered a twenty Naira note. In 1982, that was a lot of money for a hungry youth. It had more value than 2,000 Naira today. It would pay the fare back and still leave something for some food and the occasional bottle of Star beer.

There was a third encounter in the 1980s. The country had little or no jobs for its army of young men coming out of high schools or even the universities. The days were over when a job and a car awaited a university student upon graduating. As the soldier regime of the day struggled with the economy like a car with steering-wheel trouble, more and more of the youth took either to hooliganism or headless partying out of boredom. Two regimes later, one soldier 'mis-leader' would throw up his hands in frustration and declare

11

that the economy defied all scientific logic. The steering wheel had locked forever. So, one turned to the good Man for help. It was the same procedure. The difference this time was his lack of surprise in having this tender plant shooting up suddenly before his office desk.

"I need a job!"

The cheek of it! But he drew a note pad to him and scribbled a director's name and the description of a Road Safety Corps office in Ibadan. The Man himself was Chairman of the Corps.

"Give him this note; he will understand. There should be something there for you." The traditional twenty Naira note was proffered. He saved one the embarrassment this time.

In Ibadan, the director of the Road Safety Corps read the note, nodded with satisfaction and fixed an appointment, mumbling something about a clerk's job in the very near future. At the next meeting he explained that, actually, the position open was that of a 'messenger,' not a clerk's, but that the duties were practically the same; only thing was... the designation read 'Messenger'! Speechlessness. Usually the primary school drop-out was the one destined for that position, not a secondary school graduate. One's mind began to resist the devil of a messenger position. Nigerian bureaucracy never let it get past the poor obsequious messenger what a lowly foot-mat he was. Everyone wiped their feet on the doormat, some a little longer than necessary! He Sir-ed and Ma-ed even those who were the age-mates of his or her own children. No. It just would not do. So one thanked him for the offer, made noises about thinking of it and coming back with the application letter and so on, and beat a hasty retreat.

Outside the Agodi area, the buildings stared back in disbelief, the street lashed out its serpentine tongue in the direction of the Road Safety Corps office; the traffic roared, "No!" And one echoed back, "No, no, I shall be messenger to no man in Nigeria!"

Months dragged by. One found oneself standing before The Man again at Ife. This time the excuse is not rememberable. He admonished, "You should have taken the job. All you would probably have needed to do was a little bit of pen-pushing." And he mentioned how he himself was a waiter in London during his student days.

He did not know about the offer of the job of messenger instead of that of a clerk. But one said nothing of that out of fear of being seen as immodest rather than ambitious and self-respecting. More months went by, years during which his pieces of advice were implemented—reading on Radio Oyo's Youth Rendezvous, with Lekan Walker as host and producer, in 1984 (it also brought in a weekly stipend!); publishing poems in newspapers; joining the Association of Nigerian Authors in 1986 and attending its yearly conferences thereafter.

In 1989, armed with a copy of Voices from the Fringe, one walked into Akin Fashemore's office at Spectrum Books in Oluyole Industrial Estate out of curiosity and demanded a job on the spot!

"I am a poet; but I am hungry. I need a job."

The strangest of looks from him. And then compassion.

"I hope you won't bring all those your funny poet-behaviour here!"

Perhaps he referred to the nature of this meeting itself. Again, the encounter had been spontaneous. No appointment. Simply wandered into the reception area and asked for the Editorial Manager!

"No."

"And you promise not to disappoint me?" "I won't disappoint you, Sir!" "Ummm...if you promise not to disappoint me, I can create a place for you!"

The job turned out to be that of an Editorial Assistant. It is the usual entry level into the publishing industry anywhere in the world, a grey area combining the administrative (for example, coordinating the department under the Editorial Manager's supervision) with an editor's assignments—actual mark-up and copy editing, manuscript assessment, and so on.

While one was working there, Chiedu Ezeanah, a fine poet whom one had met through the University of Ibadan School of Poets, worked at the Tribune, not too far away in Oke-Ado. We sometimes met at a bar somewhere in-between Oluyole Estate and Oke-Ado. He gave news of an impending meeting of 'The Group' in Ibadan. It turned out The Group was a collective of The Man's old school mates, friends, and fellow artists like Tunji Oyelana, the high-life musician; exciting! So how would we get into Dr. Olu Agunloye's walled-in and guarded mansion in the heart of Bodija? Chiedu, as much a daredevil himself, sneered and assured one that we could get in on his journalist's pass. Great! So off we went and gate-crashed successfully on the evening. True to information, The Man was there. He arrived after we had already breached the VIP requirements of The Group's gathering; two obviously younger men among the elderly intellectual crowd. We were even allowed wine and access to the rich buffet. We had brief conversations with him and retreated into beery silences, lost in the din.

Two or three years rolled by. On a fine morning in the early 1990s, it was The Man's 56th birthday. Joop Berkhout, Chief Executive Officer and Chairman of Spectrum Books and The Man's Nigerian publisher, came into the editorial pool and searched in his bird-like fashion.

"Godwin, today you must do nothing. Drop everything. Only write a poem for Soyinka's birthday. We are going to Lagos. You will read the poem at his Birthday party." One had met The Man again when he visited Spectrum Books' offices once. He dimly remembered our encounters. Years had gone by. One was known in the company's newsletter as "our own poet" after the publication

14

of *The Faith of Vultures: BBC Prize-Winning Anthology* in 1989 by Heinemann, Oxford. Does one write to order as a baker bakes to order? Berkhout insisted. So, the employee complied and sweated out "For WS," an ode. The same evening, with no time for a change of clothes, off we went to Lagos with the boss himself driving. We had in tow a huge birthday card signed by the entire staff.

In Lagos, J.P. Clark, renowned poet and playwright, was host. Bruce Onobrakpeya, one of the country's finest visual artists, had prepared a huge canvas of some work in bronze as a birthday present. There was Anthony Kwameh Appiah in the audience. At some point, Berkhout drew the attention of the illustrious gathering through spoon against wineglass, insisting the crowd listen to a poem by Spectrum's own in-house bard. One read and was applauded, and the night roared on.

Again, there were intervening years. Then it came the time to pursue the fulfilment of a dream. Studying German language (after resigning from Spectrum Books) at the University of Ibadan required a semester or two in Germany. Self-sponsored and writing newspaper articles, TV scripts, and poetry and engaged in part-time editorial work for Gbenro Adegbola's Bookkraft, Aigboje Higo's Heinemann, one did not have enough money for three square meals, much less for an airplane ticket to Germany. Again, to the good Man. This time, he was in Abeokuta running the Essay Foundation and was not anymore with the University of Ife. Once there had been a courtesy visit to Abeokuta after the 56th birthday party, at that time to present him with the essayistic result of the birthday encounter. It was an article in the *Nigerian Tribune* titled, "Giving Wole back to Soyinka" in reference to the Onabrakpeya artwork.

An astute critic of the government's antics, The Man was under the shadow of the dictatorship of the day and had had to relocate his family, he explained, which meant buying a new home in some secret location in the country. One would have to wait till he returned from a planned international lecture tour. Then he would be able to support the German trip. He had just dusted off his forgotten lecture folder and was considering which invitations to acknowledge. On his first attempt to board a plane, the public was shocked at the news of the seizure of his passport at the Murtala Mohammed Airport in Lagos by state security officials. The next news was even more arresting. The Man had disappeared into thin air! There were rumours of a London or New York appearance. Then silence. Somehow, one managed to board a plane for Frankfurt at the end of 1994.

In 1995, years of clashes between Ken Saro-Wiwa and the government took a fatal international turn when the former was murdered by the latter. There was fevered anti-government work in Germany; anti-Shell campaigns in conference halls and on the streets alongside Uche Nduka and Elias Dunu, Peter Donatus and Ade Odukoya (BANTU), musician and Afro-German activist. The United Democratic Front was formed by The Man in the USA. The Nigerian intellectual community in Germany quickly brought itself under its umbrella. Already in place was the Nigerian Common Cause, the infrastructure and manpower of which were mobilized. Elias Dunu was at the forefront of organising. Thus, came The Man to Germany on a political mission in 1997. Conferences, talks, meetings with leaders of the EU, then he was in Cologne, home to Ade Odukoya. There was a conference. The Man gave a talk to a packed audience of German support organisations like the Association for the Protection of Threatened Peoples and the general German public. Olaokun Soyinka, who one met for the first time, was in the background, camera in hand. We had intimations that the Nigerian embassy had spies posted in the audience. We, including Ade, tried identifying and photographing them for some future 'peoples' court!' They shied away.

In the evening, at a reception in honour of The Man by the German support groups, he stood up to give a vote of thanks. One had been sitting alongside him all the while. As he began speaking, there was a slight hiss and an escape of gas as one tried opening a bottle of beer with the teeth! That was to avoid distraction by standing up to retrieve the cork-opener. He paused in his speech, turned his head slightly to take a peek at one and declared in an unbroken tone of voice to the audience, "he is one of my protégés, but I can assure you, I did not teach him how to do that!" Earlier on during the dinner, one had jokingly demanded delivery on the 1994 promise of money for a ticket to Germany! And he had replied in the same light mood, "Is it because you managed to get out!?"

Strange how fate has yoked Man and child after that initial June encounter in 1982 at the Ife University—because there were other meetings, and each time The Man was father to the child, who had not been able to be the child who is "father of the man." Again in 2001 in Düsseldorf, Germany, one was billed on a literary event focusing on Africa alongside The Man. Sheer coincidence, but one that spoke of the hand of fate, and reminded one of the challenges in that autograph of 1982, "for Godwin Ede, with sincere wishes for a successful writing career." The play, *King Baabu*, was staged in Düsseldorf in 2001. On a different billing—the poetry section—we, Uche Nduka and Godwin Ede, read poetry. Of course, it is usual now to simply seek out The Man. So, before the night of poetry, one took a train from one's home base in Hannover to Düsseldorf. Again, this time, there was an appointment. It was a courtesy call unrelated to the literary program in the city of Düsseldorf. Once more, The Man was father to the child and agreed to write a recommendation letter for a PhD program in Canada and a prospective literary grant at the New York Public Library. He took the information needed. He would post the letters back to Germany once he arrived at his base in the USA.

True to his words, generous copies of the letters were received in Hannover, Germany, a month later or thereabouts. On leaving the five-star hotel to go back to Hannover during that meeting, The Man handed the child a hundred Euro note, echoing 1982. And now the child awaits an opportunity to buy The Man his beloved wine in the very near future.

Harry and The Boys

Harry Oludare Garuba. Yes. All my names are stretched out here in this byline—much "like a patient etherized upon the table," as T.S. Elliot would have it. "Etherised"—in this case, not because I am incapacitated by a surfeit of that romantic love that is the subject of Eliot's Lovesong of J. Alfred Prufrock or that I am comatose due to the oblivion of sleep, but because I am not physically here. I have gone to another place, to other dimensions. Disembodied. So, I have decided to inhabit you like a medium, Godwin, and type with your hands but speak in my own voice. You do know my voice very well since I am in your head. You know its timbre, and tremble; its measured nuance and halting cadence; you know how to intone, name, noun, pronounce, and parrot my cigarette-piped, smoky syllables. I must warn you that I am going to ramble. It is hard to capture a whole rich life in one short conversation. So, I will just let my thoughts roam.

I will refer to you as Godwin; abeg no vex—I am just used to calling you by that according to you—ugly colonial name. You know as e be, ehn? Of course, like most departed, I am now stretched out thin as air from ear to ear, from earth to heaven upon a table that is the spirit, such that you cannot see me, and I am not anymore physically amongst "the boys." I have become an ancestor in true animist fashion. Henceforth, we can only commune in dreams. Chew seeds of alligator pepper and a bite of bitter kola nut, slug a mouthful of hot gin; do not swallow! Do not be like the swallow bird and digest but blow the brew into the air; call me in a whisper: "Harry G!" And you will hear me whisper back to you in the language of tree foliage waving in the wind; spit it into the air and intone: "Harry G," and you will see me in the winking of a sunbeam across your work table; smack your lips against the sharp taste of bitter kola nut swirling in a mouthful of hot burning gin: "Harry G," and you will see me in the smile of a cat across your path; in the murmurings of flowing rivers or—bookworm that you are—you will see my face peering at you in the tiny script of printed lettering in a book; letters that will defy logic and gravity and jump off the page to suggest esoteric meanings to you. These are omens that you should prepare for me a corner of your room for my silent, wordless dawn visits where we will commune in the language of poets and continue those University of Ibadan Student Union Building intellectual beer-laced discussions... But without the beer. Here in these new bodiless realms, I can only feed the soul, not the body. And if you look up at the dark night sky sometimes, you will see my soul in the form of a star winking and lighting up the winter or tropical night.

But make man talk true; I did enjoy myself on earth, perhaps a bit too much. You know what I mean—the great intellectual company and camaraderie for example... I remember the first time I met you, Godwin. It was probably when I was in the process of gathering poems for the first anthology of its kind in Nigeria—a generation-defining volume that became the book, *Voices from the Fringe.* This was in 1986/87, before the compendium itself came out. It is important to note that Odia Ofeimun doctored that book in his frenetic and insistent near-crowd-sourcing financial and organisational energies as the General Secretary of the Association of Nigerian Authors. He was the doctor and I, the midwife. Or well, the wife; he inseminated with project ideas and organisation, I sourced for submissions, edited, and birthed the book. You were not yet a student of the University of Ibadan at the time.

You sought me out, I think, because you had submitted your work for the forthcoming anthology that would become *Voices From the Fringe.* I was ensconced at one of the Bars in the Student Union

Building at the University of Ibadan campus as usual. Of course, we referred to building and institution respectively as 'SUB' and 'UI'. Emma Oga and Eghosa Osaghae were with me, I think. And as usual we were having some refreshments and great intellectual discussions; I was imbibing, drinking in the muses from the bottle. The Shakis flowed and the calabash in my stomach was open. It was a jolly table and an enlightened company. I cannot remember everything that we talked about, really. But I do remember that I told you that I liked your poem, titled "Song," so I was going to include it in the forthcoming anthology. I would need a bio. It was a bright afternoon further sharpened by the buzz of shakis. But you were a beam of fluorescent light shooting through an already bright day.

"Hey, how na; how are you?"

"I am fine."

"I beg, remind me of your name again."

"Godwin; 'God' for short!"

I remember chuckling at that one.

"Oniyeye!," I laughed. "'God for short'!"

And you grinned mischievously.

"I love your poem; what's the title again?"

"Song."

"Yes. I like the appeal to the primordial in it."

Back then, I had a feeling that you did not immediately intuit the indirect primordial import I was referring to in that simple short poem. This is because I could see you looking at me with surprise. But it was fine with me because historically writer and critic can never fully agree on the meaning of a text, anyway! That is why Alexander Pope in "An Essay on Criticism" chastises the critic in relationship to the writer: "Cavil you may, but never criticise!" However, and beyond obvious generalities, there are as many interpretations to a text as there are readers of that text; it is totally out of the writer's hand, out of Alexander Pope's writing hand... I was reading it as a critic, not as a poet—or perhaps as a poet-critic. But that work spoke about the "psyche [striking] up its serpent head." I read unconscious primordial instincts into that. Anyhow, I noted to you that there was an avalanche of material submitted for the anthology and that in fact a lot of them were from first-time, never-heard-of names and even by much younger emerging poets. Surprising for such a mature project. It even included submitted work from two high school girls, one—at the time—Nina Chika Uniqwe and a classmate of hers. Both were students at the Federal Government Girls College, Abuja. You marvelled. Nina's poem made it into the anthology while her classmate's did not. Nina is, of course, now the famous novelist, Chika Uniqwe. Her promise as a writer has flowered; my editorial instincts were right.

I think shortly thereafter, after our first meeting, that is—no, actually that was three years after—you began to work at Spectrum Books in Ring Road, Ibadan, as an Editorial Assistant and made sorties into UI with your company's chauffeured book delivery Kombi bus on one errand or the other, usually to make photocopies of especially unwieldy manuscripts. You would come and sit with me and the boys at the SUB, shoot breeze and then go back to work later. And you became an informal member of the Thursday group of poets at UI, sometimes coming from town to attend our poetry readings on beery Thursday evenings. And when, in 1991, you decided to formally begin studies at UI in the German department as well as in English, you simply also formalized your relationship with the UI poetry club, alias the "Thursday People." And so did you become a Thursday People yourself and properly came into my orbit, and we circulated amongst a constellation of like-minded bookish but jolly writerly characters, either students or faculty, and sometimes, like me, writer-faculty within the UI community.

The SUB was our unofficial watering hole. So respected was our space—which changed proprietorship several times but became "Alhaji's Bar"—that even when UI male cult-member-students belonging to different secret fraternities such as the Pyrates Confraternity, Eiye, Buccaneers, or Black Axe were warring with each other for juvenile respectability and street credibility, they never ventured near our hallowed drinking place. We sat there in our own mental worlds as they went on a collective rampage all over the campus, while other students were in hiding in their hostels. We refused to cede our own intellectual stomping ground and retire with tails between our legs for them to carry on their bloody gang fights. The rowdy crowd knew well enough to respect our hallowed poetic space. You would always tell me that it was because they saw in us an intellectual equivalent and ally of the streets. We were completely anti-establishment and egalitarian. You would note that I, for example, did not oppress students as a lecturer or wield the usual hierarchical 'oga-at-the-top' cudgel with which some other faculty might beat-in the heads of students. And as a group, we did not see these troubled kids as hooligans even if they were anarchic against an oppressive government and society. They were the dark side of our bright table. On one occasion, some of these boys even ran into the SUB, only to stop by for a chug of beer at our jolly table before racing out to war.

Talking of war, Godwin, you were bad once. You actually went to war alongside UI students against the Ibadan Polyethnic students, who dared to destroy some faculty property located far from the campus centre at the border between both schools. I know you did it because property belonging to innocent faculty were targeted. That afternoon, I think we were in the SUB drinking and discussing this and that. The noise was very loud about the now two-day disagreement between students of both schools. You excused yourself and disappeared. I did not see you till the next day when you came to the SUB and sat there innocently chugging beer. Then one student straggled in, saw you and turned in admiration to hail you as "commander"! The previous night, he had lain in the underbrush alongside you when the Ibadan Polytechnic students rushed and breached the border gates and were upon you all. He recalled how you had calmed him and asked him to lie low like an envelope under the darkness in the undergrowth till the wave passed. This was when Duke chastised you for such a dangerous escapade and warned you that he never wanted to hear that you ever partook in any student bickering again!

I am afraid we do not keep secrets in these outer-worldly realms, and I must say this. Your poverty as a student was legendary! Of course, you made up for it in intellectual wealth. But I remember having to call you aside from Alhaji's Bar every so often and secretly press a 100 Naira note into your hands while apologising that I knew it was small fare given the prices of goods, and also that it was hardly enough to stretch out through the hungry semester. Moreover, my own salary as a lecturer was not just mine but always shared out. But you were a good sport as you 'oh'-ed in surprise like a fish gasping for embarrassed air. Anyhow, you would intone that you could manage what I considered a paltry hundred-er and supplement it—as you had a good side hustle editing manuscripts for BookKraft and Kraft Books, as well as Heinemann Publishers. And you wrote the occasional TV script. All that while being a hardworking student. I was not even sure if you were hardworking; I just knew that you got your papers in and seemed to progress easily through your studies. I think you took only one creative writing class with me in the English department. Otherwise, your lectures were on the other side of the Faculty of Arts Quadrangle in the German department.

So, our relationship was informal—more or less that of fellow poets and 'tortured souls' whose political and existential sensitivity within the Thursday Group intellectual circle was a kind of "social cement." And whose irreverence and disregard for material things were a bafflement to those adjacent to the group—like my cousin, Theo, who was undertaking graduate studies in Economics. He loved to drop in intermittently at Alhaji's Bar to banter with us and make fun: "you these poets!"—in a manner of speaking, 'you these happily penniless poets!' And there was Mike Diai, who worked in administration. He loved to sit with us and have a pint or two. He did not care for poetry and was impatient with any formal rigid intellectualism. He derided us endlessly for writing poetry only meant to "woo women and steal people's girlfriends." He did not see the practical use or need for poetry in a tough economy. We humoured him, exchanged conspiratorial looks and laughed it off.

Duke also worked in administration and was our beloved boon companion at the jolly table. He had no use for our poetry either and seemed to shake his head at us in disapproval before buying a round for everyone. There were a lot of people—scholars, both international and local, as well as other writers from out-of-town, students, and businessmen—who over the years were revolving shadows around the Thursday Group's intellectual table. As a matter of fact, it was an academic guest from the USA who first used the expression "tortured souls" to describe some members of the group. I promptly adopted it and used it liberally—especially to capture the hypersensitivity of these frail souls, like Chiedu Ezeanah, incredible master poet but scatter-head eccentric, who hides his powerful lyrics as a squirrel hides nuts and refuses to publish and disseminate them to a larger world. I hope he has changed his ways.

I was talking about tough times back there. But somehow you financially clawed your way through the studies. You reminded me of an image in Eliot again. Somehow, your existential struggles made me think of the desperation of the poet persona in "Prufrock", who wanted to be like "a pair of ragged claws/scuttling across the floors of silent seas." The 'seas' in this case were the body of obstacles in front of you as you tried to wade your way towards Germany for further studies. I have never seen such long-suffering in one so frail! And I remember sitting with you at the SUB and ruefully advising that since you have decided on the path of exile, you cannot look back.

"You cannot put your hands to plow and look back."

"I understand."

"And you have to keep writing; you no say that's the only way we will be able to keep in touch—through our writing."

But then I did not realise that social media and telephony would explode around the world and draw in Nigeria, especially with the advent of the cell phone. MTN came into Nigeria from South Africa and universal communication became global. Years after you left, I got tired of a Nigerian system that limited research and intellectual material. Despite my great reluctance to leave the intellectual nurturing grounds of a UI that produced Wole Soyinka, Chinua Achebe, J.P. Clarke and a host of others, "I picked up my bag and left"—like Dambudzo Marechera. This is despite the fact that it was hard to tear myself from the nurture of an environment where I studied up to the PhD level and finally became a faculty member. The leave-taking seemed not to have ended for me, because from South Africa I went to the extreme and left the planet entirely, finally going back to the Source—from where I am now talking to you. I am sorry that I warned Remi Raji not to inform you of my imminent permanent departure because I knew that you, poet of the empathic steeped in the body and language of the emotive, would not be able to take it. I had to sneak away. Stay well Godwin; know that I love you as always. My regard to the boys wherever they have all scattered to; it seems to be a season of migrations. I am very much alive here, waiting for all of you to come home, have a drink with me here and talk celestial poetry.

Ulli Beier: A Pagan Yoruba Man in Christian Bayreuth

Ifly from Lagos to Frankfurt straight into the winter breath of December in 1994. Huffing and puffing my way across Germany for the next several months, I end up in Bayreuth in 1995 to pursue a one-year German language intensive preparatory class towards full-blown studies. It is here in this sleepy university town, which speaks a drowsy and guttural low German, that I learn from Paul Onovoh, Nigerian PhD candidate at Bayreuth University, that there is a Yoruba man in town who lives in a residence aptly referred to as 'Iwalewa Haus.' He is White and his name is Ulli Beier. Of course, Beier (also known as Obotunde Ijimere) is so detribalised that I do not think of him as German, any more than I consider Susanne Wenger Austrian. Wenger, a boon companion of Beier's earlier years, initially came to Oshogbo with him around 1950 and never left, remaining in that small western Nigerian town as an Osun devotee and later priestess for the rest of her life.

I find it amusing that I think of beer when I hear the familiar name, Beier. Perhaps this is mere phonetic and visual accident, due to a lifelong habit of pronouncing and reading English even as I engage in serious graduate-level German? But there is playful mischief involved. My overactive imagination adds a truly 'local' colour. Everyone knows that Bayern is notorious for its annual Oktoberfest—that gay and sunny communal drink-fest full of beer and bratwurst, where Bacchus himself would feel completely at home. Beer. Ulli Beier. I cannot believe he lives in this dusty, moat-eaten town; why not neighbouring glamorous Munich, sophisticated

Frankfurt, picturesque Bonn, or world–renowned Berlin? I am giddy while mispronouncing his name. The drunken feeling evoked does not come from Oktoberfest beer draughts served by those rumoured big-bosomed, Amazon German waitresses with matronly girdles. It is rather due to Beier's legendary exploits as an astute promoter, pioneer, and bedrock of modern Nigerian culture from the time of dinosaurs—when literary and arts patronage was not fashionable across Africa.

In the colonial-era-dawning of modern Nigerian literary and visual arts, Beier— himself a writer—did not only act as the usual expatriate literary critic, educator, and scholar, but also as patron, facilitator, curator, translator, anthologist, publisher, and mentor to then-fledgling writers like Chinua Achebe, Wole Soyinka, Christopher Okigbo and Mabel Segun and dramatists like Duro Ladipo. His Mbari club, spanning 1961-1967—which was echoed in his Mbari-Mbayo Art centre in Oshogbo and its gallery of early Oshogbo Art School visual artists—was an important cultural watering hole for foundational Nigerian writers, as well as a bridgehead linking early Nigerian literary activities to continental and metropolitan fashions and movements. Through his cultural networking and promotional activities, he inserted modern Nigerian cultural production into 20th century post-war liberating and anti-colonial energies. That was within the atmosphere of a phenomenon scholars now refer to as Black Internationalism as it was exemplified and practised within the Negritude Movement, Harlem Renaissance, and Indigenism in Paris, New York, and Latin America and the Caribbean respectively. The Mbari Movement, co-founded in Ibadan by Ulli Beier, can be added to that complex. Living in the same town with this genie and breathing the same air is quite overpowering. I decide to seek Beier out, shake hands with history and be done with it.

Iwalewa Haus is in the 'Stadtmitte'—that is, at the heart of Bayreuth, around the outer perimeters of a busy inner-city central bus terminal and the hospitality and shopping district. Far enough away from the madding crowd, it sits right on the lip of windswept, narrow Münzgasse Street, number 9, with just a narrow sidewalk separating it from the occasional traffic. It is a nondescript, leaf-veined block of building perched on a narrow, slightly winding incline. The façade carries the timeworn and famous sign, IWALEWA HAUS, vertical and aslant away from the front door with which it forms a 90-degree angle. Except for that sign, the murals on the walls outside, and the carved wood doors, the building can easily pass for the residence of an eccentric graffiti artist. Only when you enter is there a suggestion that this is a veritable institution built over a half century across many countries in sub-Saharan Africa and finally housed here in a small, quiet German town.

I press the doorbell. Georgina Beier, the woman of the house, opens the double street doors with a smile. I am expected. She leads me into the foyer, up a staircase to the main level of the house and a hallway which appears to be an art gallery, albeit one where nothing seems to be for sale. Creating the atmosphere of a permanent exhibition, large paintings and adire and batik cloth adorn the walls and sculptures dot the hallway. There is no real furnishing; it is mostly exhibition space in the corridor and in the adjoining rooms, with the occasional office workstation. As I later discover on subsequent visits, it is the same on all of three floors except, perhaps, for the uppermost, which is also the living quarters for Ulli and Georgina.

I take a seat on one of the occasional cane chairs or benches lying around the rather empty exhibition hall while Georgina disappears into the upper levels of the house. While I wait for Beier, I decide to explore. I stand up and move from room to room, a lone guest at an expansive exhibition. I note that the paintings are reminiscent of the Oshogbo School: they are replete with traditional Yoruba motifs, religious and otherwise. Some Igbo influences are discernible too. But it is disproportionately a collection of Yoruba art. In short, Iwalewa Haus, from all appearances, is a gallery of mostly Yoruba painting and artwork, interspersed with work from Eastern Nigeria and other parts of the continent. While I am in contemplation, I hear a voice at the door. It is Beier. We proceed to an office off the hallway where we can sit across from each other and have a conversation.

He is of a slight, well-kept built, average height, and grey-headed. His seeming frailty is that of a taut bow. I can feel the resilience and energy in his frame. And the eyes are keen as blades and penetrating, yet with a soft and wise film over them. We make small talk before he suddenly lets off a sharp arrow out of his bow: "Why do Nigerians run after foreign gods when they have traditional models aplenty—like the Orisha religion?" It is a sobering thought, which invokes another time, another place, and a different mental space.

We enter a pagan time capsule and are shut out of a suffocating Christian evangelical Bayreuth, and Germany. Without referring to her, he has invoked the person of Susanne Wenger, a good pagan, with his remark—recalling Oshogbo and their work together there in another life. It occurs to me that he has never really left Nigeria spiritually. The essence of Oshogbo and its ambience is recreated in the paintings and artwork collected at Iwalewa Haus; their religious undertones are a form of communion and devotional service to the Osun Oshogbo grove where such artworks are represented in their sacred form in stone sculptures, and where Wenger is still artist in residence and Osun priestess, carrying on in their behalf, while he devotes himself to the secular, scholarly, and deceptively mundane—such as Iwalewa Haus.

A pagan Yoruba religious and social worldview is captured in the compressed axiomatic substantive, 'Iwalewa'—literally meaning 'character is beauty,' and (in its expanded adjectival form) 'only those who have character are truly beautiful.' 'Iwa,' character, is a necessity for any true devotee of pagan Yoruba religion, whether it is of the Ifa or Osun variety. In Ifa, this phenomenon is referred to as 'Iwapele,' synonymous with 'iwalewa.' At one point in our conversation, he emphasises this with an anecdote.

When Beier arrived in Ibadan in the early 1950s to take up a teaching appointment at the Extra Mural Studies Department of what was then the University College, according to him, Ibadan was mostly rural. People were so pure-hearted in their pagan devotion—honest, true and beautiful—that he never needed to remove the ignition key from his car, the doors of which he also left open sometimes. No one would steal the car. He could leave it at any spot in that town all day and it would be waiting when he got back. Such is the purifying strength of Yoruba religion. The moral he is pointing at is that those were the days of innocence, that with the modern desertion of Yoruba religion, such purity of character, that 'iwalewa,' has also deserted the average Yoruba, or Nigerian by extension.

Iwalewa Haus itself, as a cultural centre, is then a reminder of the requirements for a true pagan devotee of Yoruba religion; a kind of religious grove, a place of worship, with Beier as its priest if we go by the example of his life. 'Iwalewa' as a Yoruba religious axiom and requirement for worship sums up the esoteric dimension of Beier's cultural work, which, through the beauty of his character, transcends race, language, geographies, gender, and all other material and limiting suffocations, such as popular modern religion, politics, and other kinds of shortness of sight.

I sit there as Beier's vision of pagan ritual and liturgy unfolds. I do not need much convincing from this detribalised, White Yoruba man in Germany wearing a traditional tie-dye shirt. The proof is in his life, spread out before me like an Ifa divination chain. Through honest, pagan vigour he will found the Mbari-Mbayo Literary and Arts Movements, without which the history of modern Nigerian literary culture would be the poorer. It is an occasion for rejoicing because Ulli Beier is not dead but has merely joined his pagan Yoruba ancestors.

Austin Clarke—Darkness Visible
(a posthumous interview)

Amatoritsero Ede: I have always wanted to have an interview with you, Mr. Clarke. I kept postponing it. I once asked Dr George Elliot Clarke, your brother from another father, I guess—since you share the same last name—if he could introduce me, which he promised to do. But I never got back to the subject with him because I got distracted by one thing or the other. Unfortunately, I was not fast enough before the grim reaper knocked on your door. I did not realize that he was so close by you. I apologize profusely. Fortunately, in my days as a monk in another world, I did learn some esoteric arts. I decided to use some occult knowledge to travel the astral world and meet you on the other side for this interview. Surely, you don't mind an outer-worldly, out-of-body chat, do you?—on earth this would be considered a posthumous interview.

Austin Clarke: Quite the opposite, Amatoritsero, I don't mind an interview in the fourth or even fifth or sixth dimension. Are we in the fifth?

A.E.: Our world...my world...is three dimensions—length, breadth, and solid. Since you—your soul—has left your physical body (no one ever dies, of course) you moved out of those material dimensions and are now in a fourth and bodiless and invisible one, I believe. That is, if you have not progressed to even higher levels. Yes, you are not limited by gross matter anymore. Not by colour, come to think of it, which can be as heavy as any form of matter.

A.C.: That is why WEB DuBois correctly predicted that the problem of the 20th century would be that of 'the colour line.' His brother, Alain Locke, in *The New Negro*, insisted that the colour line will persist throughout the 21st century. Colour is indeed heavy as an unnecessarily racialized quality—heavy as a winter coat that burdens you and impedes you, even when you do need the melanin as environmental protection. This is why I was such a reluctant Canadian.

A.E.: I was going to get to the subject of your reticence in taking a Canadian citizenship. But first. How is it out here in 'Vaikunta'; do you feel claustrophobic, not being in our world, in the great wide-open plains of Canada and the large expanse of—?

A.C: You make me laugh a Barbadian laugh! Your world is so tiny, like a grain of sand on an endless seashore. Look at all material creation, including earth and the galaxies. They are almost limitless. But the Bhagavad Gita, one of the Hindu Scriptures, says all that material creation is like a little blot, a tiny stain, on the spiritual sky. Imagine the vastness, magnificence, and infinitude of spiritual creation. Those earthly expanses you talk of cannot be compared to the freedom of being unfettered, bodiless. "Poor wordless body in its fumbling ways," as the South African poet, Dennis Brutus, says. Having no body and no colour, because of which spiritually ignorant humans vilify and demonise you, is a great experience. By the way, is Vaikunta not the final resting place of the soul, according to the Bhagavad Gita?

A.E.: Yes, it is. When you need not reincarnate anymore as a living entity because you have learnt all the spiritual lessons which you needed in a human body, you rise to Vaikunta as a spirit soul in pure worship of the godhead – Krishna, Christ, Allah—or any other name we humans call it/him/her in our usual divisive lack of understanding that the godhead may be many but is one and the same, no matter how we differently name the idea.

A.C.: Ah…! I am not sure I want to reincarnate and come to your world anymore. Those 81 years in your world (or prison) had better be my last incarnation—or is it incarceration! I brek-up from racism, sexism, ageism, war, injustice, especially brek-up from dispossession and lack of privilege due to my Blackness—

A.E.: Excuse me Mr. Clarke, sir. But you were privileged!

A.C.: Amatoritsero Ede! I think you are being a devil's advocate here. My foot biting me! You see, I was not privileged at all, or rather what appeared to be privileged—my success as a writer, my access to print capital, was fought for every inch of the way. I suffered lack because of it and the typical writer's poverty. Rather, what I was in your world was "Darkness visible," to pun the English poet, John Milton. And don't call me 'Clarke'; that's a human name… Call me 'Guru Hari Das.' I am now the servant of the servant of the servant of the godhead in these realms.

A.E.: Guru Hari Das! Okay. But for the purpose of this interview…please. Yes, "darkness visible"… I know of that oxymoron from Milton's *Paradise Lost.* It is in chapter one of that work about the fall of man.

A.C.: For argument's sake, one could say I had some empowerment towards the end. But it was at that time that death came with his dark hood and sickle for me… In my old age, at the time when a valiant warrior should be enjoying the fruits of his labours. Now if I were White, at any age I'd have been really privileged. My successes would have catapulted me to unimaginable places, brought incredible wealth, and so on… Imagine…at the foot of the fire, when I should be in my salad days, death comes fi me.

A.E: Would you like to reincarnate as a White man so that you could experience the privilege of Whiteness?

A.C.: By my beard! At'all. No! I am not a black hat. I can't be enjoying while others suffer. This was why I was an activist.

A.E.: Beard? But you are bodiless!

A.C.: I mean by the grey heavy beard and lion mane I used to wear on earth.

A.E.: Yes, your activism in the 60s. Interviewing Malcom X for CBC and all that. Civil rights marches. That was something... Did you meet the soul of Malcom X since you arrived here?

A.C.: Blasted! Those were the days of struggle. I have not felt that soul around my soul. That jolly troublemaker on earth must be in Vaikunta already.

A.E.: What is the context when you say above that you are "darkness visible"? Although, I think I get it, but for our readers, you know...?

A.C: I use it in a literal and symbolic sense. I am 'physically visible' because I am Black and invisible within Canadian society. Ironic da! I mean my visibility made me a known corporeal category that the system makes sure to avoid, impede, hold back, keep in the ghetto, deny rights, deny opportunities, mis-educate, manipulate with 'Canadianspeak' (that polluted 'political correctness' and 'polite' conversation that mocks me, derides me, looks down upon me, and puts me in 'my place')! I am over-controlled and checked and checked again and again. The system disappears my kind. Darkness visible. I am Ralph Ellison's invisible man precisely because they look at me but do not see me. They only see darkness (i.e., nothing). They do not see me when it comes to housing opportunities, job opportunities; they impeded my kind by asking me for Canadian experience when I am just coming in from another world into theirs. And you know the greater irony? It is no one's fault. Fuh-true? Kwablema! We are multicultural and one great family of Canadians! All equal. But as George Orwell is my witness, all Canadians are equal, but some Canadians are more equal than others. I also use "darkness visible" to capture the hellish conditions that Mr. John Milton uses to describe souls suffering in Hades. It is the Black or Brown man or woman catching hell on earth. Please bear with me and let me quote:

> A dungeon horrible, on all sides round
> As one great Furnace flam'd, yet from those flames
> No light, but rather darkness visible
> Serv'd onely to discover sights of woe,
> Regions of sorrow, doleful shades, where peace [65]
> And rest can never dwell, hope never comes
> That comes to all; but torture without end
> Still urges, and a fiery Deluge, fed
> With ever-burning Sulphur unconsum'd:
> Such place Eternal Justice had prepar'd [70]

Amatoritsero, in the above quote Milton is talking about the rebellious angel Lucifer ('angel of light') who was called 'Satan' after the rebellion and was cast down from heaven into the hell that the poet, Milton, so vividly paints above. When man falls, he joins Satan in that hell too. Replace Satan with the Black man... from slavery to colonialism and the current imperial moment in humanity, the Black man or woman has been demonized, be-devil-ed, and satanized the better for him or her to be cast into a fire of suffering and servitude on earth. The last line above says: "Such place Eternal Justice had prepared." Replace "Eternal Justice" with 'Eternal injustice' against Blackness and you get my drift.

A.E.: Blasted! This is all heavy! Thank you for the elaborate explanation; I am sure our readers appreciate it.

A.C.: Blasted indeed! Colour is heavy. Sorry I had to heap it all on you like that.

A.E.: What a life of it you must have had. Must have been irritating and annoying!

A.C.: They make an awful ruka-tuk about me being a Black Panther and all that. I was simply a freedom fighter! The 60s especially was either fight or die! If you complain you are an "angry Black man."

A.E.: You wrote this in your memoir, *Membering* (2015): "I am living… in the sixties, in the atmosphere of great physical fear, of the expectation that a policeman might shoot me—bang, bang, you're dead, dead—of being refused the renting of a basement room, or an apartment in a public building, that I would find myself standing noticeably longer than other customers at a counter in Eaton's store, at the corner of Yonge and College Streets, that I might be thrown out, sometimes physically, from a restaurant, or a nightclub, as Oscar Peterson was, and face the embarrassment of being told by a barber that he does not cut niggers' hair. This is my Toronto." Has anything changed over the years?

A.C.: The only thing that changed is that the system has developed better ways to hide racial prejudice and injustices.

A.E.: The Cultural commentator, Donna Bailey Nurse, says of you: "When I think of Austin Clarke, I think of how his fiction irrevocably etched West Indians, Bajans, Black people, and himself into the landscape of Toronto and the collective imagination of Canadians. I think of the courage with which he exposed to White people the psychological realities of being Black in the world." What is the psychological reality of being Black in the world, in Canada precisely?

A.C.: I think I am going to answer by saying that general White Canada does not understand the pressures, hopes, fears, and anxieties of Black Canada. One commentator put it well—Doug

Sanders in The Globe and Mail of July 16, 2016. He compares it to the situation Blacks face in the USA. I refer to his article "Why Black Canadians are facing U.S.-style Problems": See it at: http:// www.theglobeandmail.com. But the article adopts a justice-system-critique approach. I will talk from a more overarching cultural vantage point. There is a silent marginalization of not only Black people but the immigrant community too—right from when they come in... Remember one of our past governments hierarchizing immigrants as second-order Canadians? I think that says it all. In officialspeak we are all Canadians, but in terms of the ways in which institutional and official bureaucracies and the general culture actually work, visible minorities are on the fringe of society. They are economically marginalized; they are socially marginalized in terms of not being properly integrated into White society; they are forced to mostly re-create the home they left by seeking Jamaican, Bajan, Nigerian, Ghanaian, Indian, South African etc. communities to attach themselves to. Politically, I am not sure if they have any real impact as a collective group. The shortfall is that those marginalized immigrants and Black Canadians cannot contribute all their talents and resources to the nation. Canada as a country loses.

A.E.: In your memoir you wrote, "I have never held a Canadian writer as a model of my own work. This is simply because the theme and the style of Canadian literature are irrelevant to my work. I do not therefore see any connection, in the sense of 'literary ancestry,' to my writing. I am alone, singular, peculiar, and foreign to the establishment that governs and controls Canadian literature." Do those words mean that you felt alienated even while living in Canada all those years? Words do come to haunt.

A.C.: I like the ghosts of these words because they are true. I was an insider-outsider... My writing drew sustenance from my Caribbean experiences even though I began living in Canada on

September 29, 1955. You must also have read somewhere that I delayed taking a Canadian citizenship until 1981. This reflected my ambivalence. Barbadian-Canadian; split down the middle, but with one side torn more towards the Barbadian left than the right that Canada can sometimes be.

A.E.: So, this the reason your former publisher, Patrick Crean, says that your work was "an early example of the literature of diversity and displacement, a quality that now informs our literature." He also says that your "influence was huge," that your work "broke the mould of White Canada"—specifically in relation to your first book in 1964, *Survivor of the Crossing*. What writers of colour would you say you have influenced?

A.C.: David Chariandy, Esi Edugyan, Shyam Selvadurai, Rohinton Mistry, M.G. Vassanji... to name a few. Don't get me wrong, those influences might not be very direct—as in the case of writers who are closer to, or not too far apart from, my earthly age before I left the body. I am thinking of Mistry and Vassanji, who are contemporaries. However, contemporaries still do influence each other. I opened the floodgates, so to speak. As for the younger writers, Edugyan particularly... Just read the electric and jazzy vernacular in her powerful *Half-Blood Blues* and you will clearly see the influence of *The Polished Hoe*.

A.E.: You opened the floodgates you say... See why I said you were privileged?

A.C.: Ah, come off it, Amatoritsero. You mekin' sport. I am darkness made visible as I have said with all the punning intended. Being literary-visible did not remove my 'darkness' and all the accursed Freudian symbology attached to it and to my being a Black man in a White world. Literary celebrity only made me a token—I was the exception to a 'keep-dem-down' rule, an example to be pointed at as proof of the fairness of a system rigged against the coloured immigrant. Remember that sealed and deadly reference letter (meant for employment purpose in White America), which an—ironically—Black school principal gave to the Black protagonist in Ralph Ellison's *Invisible Man*? It said without flourish: "To whom it may concern; keep this Nigger boy running." I was just a token.

A.E.: But there are new minority writers coming along as you have noted. Maybe things are changing. I mean Chariandy, Edugyan, Shyam... younger generation...

A.C.: They are part of that token few. Look at the numbers. Go to any Canadian writers' festival and count the coloured writers you see as invited guests. They are token and few.

A.E.: Finally, I would like to ask you to lighten up the prospects. Some word of hope. What advice do you have for Black or immigrant communities, especially young writers trying to thrive under the conditions you so eloquently painted for us?

A.C.: I am out of it. I did my part. I would say it like Bob Marley and Peter Tosh did: "Get up; stand up; don't give up the fight!"

A.E.: But...

A.C.: Okay; okay, oh lordie! I did not mean they should join the Black Panthers or things like that. Self-help, group help, community building, education by hook or crook, economic self-reliance. Start businesses, support each other; solidarity. Don tear the family down through 'crab-in-the-bucket' behaviour, the PhD (pull-him-down). Remember that song by the Toronto musician, k-os— *Crabbukit*? Aluta continua!

A.E.: MTLS, our readers and I would like to really thank you for giving me audience in the spiritual realm to have this chat. Rest in peace, maestro.

A.C.: I am rested and peaceful already. My soul is liming here.

I have gone into the light. It is you on earth who live in the darkness of Kali Yuga and have no peace. Sadly, you all live in an age of ignorance and quarrel. That is the nature of Kali Yuga.

A.E.: Thank you. Bye for now, my astral body must now re-enter my physical body before my silver cord breaks and I cannot re-enter or realign well.

A.C.: Hurry. Good luck. You don't want to kartspraddle into your physical body.

Face Me; I Book You!:
The Arts and Asocial Media

"If the poet can no longer speak for society,
but only for himself, then we are at the last ditch."
– Henry Miller

I remember setting up a Facebook profile with great reluctance a few years ago. I did not put up a single picture there for two years, and I screened myself off with a pseudonym. Otherwise, any evil eye could peep into my soul or sitting room at will through the window of social media—never mind the much-vaunted self-protection modules on the site. All it would take is a hacker-style breach of all privacy protocols. Still, "resistance is futile" in the age of social media, particularly if you need it as a tool or do not want to risk ending up as a 21st century Luddite.

My creative activities eventually unmasked me, and I am now a regular denizen of that cyber world even though I inhabit that space strictly for its utility. But a recent strange encounter from the most unexpectedly irritating of sources—another creative writer— confirms my suspicions in ways far in excess of my original worries and leads me to question the artist's sense of social commitment in an age of "global babble."

Before going into the details of the macabre encounter, I want to elaborate on the reasons for my initial aversion to social media because it has import for the event itself. Apart from possible unbidden intrusions, there is the tendency for great miscommunication due to 'interference,' where messages, instant or not, get twisted en route, especially without the mediation of a face-to-face. Another irritant is the twin staple of vanity and narcissism deriving from the manic self-importance reflected off the mirror of social media. This sickening, almost perverse self-love is further exaggerated by that insidious illusion of instant familiarity called the 'friends list.' While all these can reduce the full-grown adult to a blubbering, self-worshipping infant and egomaniac, it also leaves room for unwarranted abuse, harassment, intimidation, and bullying or cowardly attacks from behind an impersonal computer monitor. The last is precisely what I suffered in a surreal encounter this past week at the hands of a pretend friend and Internet Tiger—apologies to Pius Adesanmi—on Facebook.

I must say I had completely buried my social media phobia and was oblivious till the devil himself violently tapped me on the shoulder with his spiked trident: "You're an asshole, Amatoritsero, a total, fucking and complete asshole. Fuck you and everything you stand for. Fuck you. Fuck you. Fuck you." Those are the devil's deranged words in a private Facebook message to a 'virtual' stranger. Let us keep in mind that I have never met him in real life, never had any conversation beyond a few hellos across the ether in several years. I do not know how to react to this bolt from the daemonic blue and wonder if it is not an example of that miscommunication of which I have been wary. Otherwise, I seriously suspect that this apparently high-strung writer might be on drugs. 'Give the devil the benefit of the doubt,' I think. 'He may be coming down from a hard dose of cocaine or has had a bad day in hell.' So, I ask him calmly:

"Why this unwarranted attack; I am mystified?"

And he responds sharply:

"I only say to you here in a private message what I could not say to you in public. The so-called 'attack' is due to your insularity. How can you not know Khezia Jones!"

This is when I remember that several hours earlier and for the first time ever, I wrote on the devil's Facebook wall, asking him who the artist in a video still he posted a short while earlier was. His irritated response had been: "Keziah Jones, of course! Google him. Don't tell me you don't know Keziah Jones!" Now in light of the vicious verbal assault in a private message, I wonder why, if at all, I need to know Khezia Jones, who seems to be the devil's alter ego.

I turn to my horned 'friend' himself for answers. I examine his life and work. He is Nigerian, like his alter ego, the musician. Both of them are expatriated—my wicked antagonist in the UK and the other in France. The one common bond between both is that they are vicarious entertainers. Apart from writing fiction, the devil struts his stuff on the stage like the musician does. Both are theatrical. And what this kind of absurd theatre does is to merely entertain in a world going through paroxysms–a tumultuous Middle East, racism, the Israel/Palestine debacle, a wayward global economy, environmental pollution, and the threat of extinction from nuclear proliferation. Not in any of the devil's novels or plays do I find a tissue of social conscience. A huge moral hole plunges through his writings. As for his alter ego's music, surely it does not have the firebrand activism of a Fela or the philosophical depth of a Bob Marley. These kinds of art are Sunday distractions for somnambulist petit bourgeoisie; transient art which, like bubble gum, is chewed, enjoyed, and spat out.

It became clear to me that my interlocutor is that kind of writer with a split personality, who cultivates the public persona of the carefully groomed romantic artist, dreadlocks and all, while in secret he is nothing but a sadistic sociopath. Yes, he made sure to throw his tantrum in secret behind the wall of a private Facebook message and not in public. This dreadlocked nightmare reminded me of Arthur Rimbaud, whose schizophrenia was captured in the incongruence of his sublime poetry and his dealing in slaves and gunrunning in Harar, Ethiopia, in the late1800s. The only difference being that Rimbaud's dissolution was public, not private.

It might seem strange to compare gunrunning and slave raids— both depraved and criminal in Rimbaud (slavery had been abolished in Europe at the time)—with the devil's bipolar behaviour. Nevertheless, the fact is that his meltdown is only the first sign of a more serious pathology and could lead in any direction of future depravity. Rimbaud's dissolution took time. And the dissimulation (hiding behind a private message) involved in the devil's behaviour is particularly typical of psychopaths, who are highly intelligent, but usually very cunning, appearing quite harmless and are apparently well-integrated members of society. It is the Dr. Jerkyll and Mr. Hyde syndrome.

Rimbaud's schizophrenia was the occasion for Henry Miller's critique in *The Time of the Assassins*. In the epigraph above from Miller's critique, the 'poet' refers to Rimbaud in the latter's abdication of his social responsibility as artist when he became degenerate but, more importantly, in the sense of societal betrayal and his dark, Jekyll-and-Hyde personality. It is instructive that the devil was first and foremost a poet. But poetry deserted him as it deserted Rimbaud the slaver and gunrunner in the end. Although in reality the devil deals in words, not in slaves or guns, the aggregate lack of social cohesion in those words (those plays and novels), of which his secret Facebook attack is a symptom, all point to the same brooding, sociopathic personality Rimbaud needed to deal in slaves or arms. Beyond Miller's particular reference to Rimbaud, I deploy 'poet' here to collectively refer to those—writers, musicians, painters, or artists generally—whose calling requires sensitivity and compassion as a unit of social engagement in their work and in their personal comportment.

For a writer to secretly attack with words on Facebook is to turn it into asocial media; it is to abdicate the social roles of the artist as the conscience of society, as the example of elevated humanity for the politician, the soldier, and the plebeian. The devil's work, with its empty noise and entertainment value (novel after novel, play after play, story after story), merely adds to the global babble in the world. It leaves the world deaf from that noise, deprives it of the ability to reflect, and makes it incapable of meditating or socially mediating for solutions. While it entertains, a work must remember to elevate, or if it does elevate, then the writer's life must not cancel out his work as Rimbaud's life did his poetry. The devil's bipolar personality profoundly complicates any future hope of that empathy that is at the heart of the socially committed writer's trade. We are indeed "at the last ditch," as Miller says of Rimbaud, "when the poet no longer speaks for society" but for his own selfish goals—in the devil's case, that of mere economic survival every theatre season, cheque by royalty cheque and grant for grant.

Cultural Critique

End of the American Empire

The very title of this think piece is an exaggeration, appropriately and deliberately so. The, at the time, new and bloated Orwellian American presidency was an excess of indecorum; official doublespeak; political ignorance, naivety, arrogance, and gerrymandering; race-and-religion-baiting; national sectarian divides and international diplomatic catastrophes. In short, that misgovernment was a painful and embarrassing abscess—a swollen boil on the world's pubic region.

While the informing sentiment here might also appear to be an exaggeration, it only captures the equally hyperbolic political wish of that then new America to self-destruct—quite without the aid of any terrorists, ironically—to implode and disintegrate rather quickly instead of aging, waning, and melting away like all Empires do. In that contradictory Yankee instance, there was the possibility of a sudden-death syndrome to be brought about by a bungling, immature, ego-maniacal Whitehouse trapped in the Lacanian mirror stage of child development. It was a special never-seen kind of childish Whitehouse whose forearms flailed and fluttered—face, neck, and mouth askew—in a derisive and inhumane mimicry of a disabled American journalist during the political primaries campaign. The twisted mouth of that campaign went on to spew more political vomit in the infancy and infantilism of that administration. In the grip of the disease of the mouth, that regime reeled from one verbal scandal to another, tweet-by-insane-tweet, splintering the American body politic further, alienating allies abroad, inflaming the world and eroding

America's global, moral, and political standing—all within a tiny fraction of the usual probationary hundred days!

The core instinct and ethic of that bipolar regime was disdain for the other and an official dissimulation to sustain it. This was keeping in with America's founding egotism—American interest above all interests. And in that regard, who was defined as 'American' was ultimately (de)based on the same othering disdain and spite, which, in its most vitriolic form, escaped out as the murderous actions of an unrepentant Dylan Roof. America's political death wish was the result of that unthinking, headless racism. What else could have brought an alt-right-post-truth-alternative-facts-President to power if not an insidious and cancerously benign racism couched in the language of shameless self-interest, rabid nationalism, and of securing a 'homeland' that actually consists of mainly immigrants—except for the indigenous (First-Nation) Native American. That racism is the shifty bedrock of a shaky American Empire; it has been eating away and corroding the body politic like acid from the moment the first slave ship docked in Virginia in 1619. This historical fact—the docking, enslavement, and flagellation of Black bodies—planted the seeds of the alt-right-White-right poisonous fruit that America has always been devouring and which makes her sick and now, retch. The plant of that sad fruit, which is bitter and sweet at the same time depending on who is chewing on what part of it, has been watered by over two centuries of wilful blindness to its realpolitikal and social health hazards.

In recent history, an American decline in global power was set in motion not so much by the events of September 11, 2001, as by the disproportionate, arrogant, and unmeasured military responses to it. These depleted state coffers, dismembered troop limbs, shattered combatant lives, demoralized bereaved families, and became the distant but immediate precursor of a U.S. bankruptcy in 2008, with its accompanying global financial meltdown. The regime that succeeded those wars of self-depletion helped to roll back that decline and set the country on its original course towards a lasting imperium. However, that new government again rewound the clock, moving the hand of retrogression rapidly forward. An isolationist and a protectionist new dispensation could only whittle down the remaining prestige and power of this dying giant, till the country is carved, shaved, and paired into a flute for blowing tunes of rapid decline, failure, and diminishing global power.

That erstwhile new regime was a personification of the proverbial hubris and arrogance that precedes a fall. Hubris it was indeed for America to deny its history and bury the dead rotting thing, that succubus of hate and barbarism called racism; to embalm the living smelly corpse with the cloth of manifest destiny and assume there is no such thing as karma. The very thing that could have kept the imperium longer, namely internal group cohesion, was sacrificed for sectional, racialized interests. It is an age-old truism that a house divided cannot stand. America was embattled at home, and abroad it drew awkward stares reserved for the terminally ill. The empire is dying!

However, that Government's narrative was that America was being made great right now. It was a new squeaky-clean, non-racist progressive nation with its eyes set on a horizon of greatness and renewed vigour—even when clearly this was a troubled country breathing its last sighs into the yawning pits and on the verge of 'ruin-nation.' Considering that country's founding self-declaration as a bastion of freedom and democracy, George Orwell probably never had America in mind when he wrote his anti-fascist novel, *1984*. However, fascism was abroad, swaggering along Whitehouse corridors in blue suit and red tie; it was clean shaven, rotund, well-fed; incredibly petulant and full of tantrums like a spoilt little boy. More than just turning in his grave, the British Orwell must have been doing backflips in alarm at his American cousins.

That regime reminds one of the over-wise and self-deflationary cunning of the Tortoise in Yoruba folktales. Noting that her husband, the Tortoise, is dressed up to the nines to embark once again on another of his unending shenanigans, Yannibo, the wife and moral conscience in the tale, asks plaintively: "IJapa, my husband, this journey you are embarking on again, when are you going to return?" Ijapa throws his flowing gowns around him in a celebratory flourish and bells out a response in a dancing singsong: "Not until I have been disgraced, disgraced, disgraced; not until I have been disgraced!" The then new American government was the Tortoise in the tale; it embarked on a journey from which it would not return until Empire had been disgraced.

The Language of Stupid

Africa has been in trouble since 1441, when the Portuguese sailors, Antão Gonçalves and Nuno Tristão, "threw down rusted anchor" in Cabo Branco on the coast of modern Mauritania, went on land, collared 12 Africans like wild game, decked them down into the rotten holes of a pirate ship and chain-ganged them into Portugal as chattel slaves. The captured men could have been specimen of some hibernating genus to be quickened into brutal medieval 'new-world' life in a culturing of slaps, kicks, branding with hot iron like cattle, lashes from horsewhips; slave auctions and unpaid back-breaking donkey's labour in inclement weather for 400 years. In other words, those initial kidnapped 12 were articles of 'the wicked trade.' That was terrorism at its most bestial.

As a matter of course, that Neanderthal continental ransacking and plunder, euphemistically explained off as a "slave trade," was not considered evil as long as it suited nascent capitalist interests in the old Western Church and State. Even a sitting pope winked and gave a sly carefree nod! He has a name too—Nicholas V. His two wild and raging Bulls—the *Dum Divas* of 18 June 1452 and the *Romanus pontifex* of 8 January 1454—further gored an already impaled medieval Africa with steely, illegal horns called papal decrees. They gave legitimacy to an ongoing criminal act, the chattel-enslavement of 'non-Christians'—in the medieval church's understanding, non-humans.

The deep-etched scars of Africa's initial encounter with a "wild-wild West" runs long and thin into the present because those 400 years of the physical and symbolic flagellation of Black bodies continues apace by other disguised and 'democratic' means today. Such trickeries could be in the form of Western economic aid packages that belie Africa-hostile fiduciary policies, such as IMF loans that are booby traps of eternal continental indebtedness; or the oxymoron of imperialist Western military interventions alongside (an apparently benevolent but alienating) cultural programming, with their artistic prize awards—this is, to the discerning, bread and bullets. All of that is ironically enabled by a greedy contemporary and comprador African political leadership that forgets its peoples' history as people. It is only such forgetting that can explain the ongoing surreptitious symbolic re-colonizing of African land by China in collusion with an African Union giddy with kickbacks and bribery. Of course, those who forget their history will repeat it. Counting from 1441 to 2022, that local, wilful, politico-historical amnesia becomes 581 years of idiotic African leadership; it will amount to 6 whole centuries of monumental Stupidity in 2041.

Stupidity has been in display across time in, and about, Africa from all manner of different actors—institutions, groups, or individuals, both local and global, insiders and outsiders, well-wishers and antagonists; as well as from friend and foe alike. One stupid friend comes readily to mind—the missionary, Albert Schweitzer, who insisted that "the African is indeed my brother but my junior brother"; that is, subordinate and unequal. Ironically, the strangest Stupid was first remarkably displayed amongst those politically naive and egoistic slave-trading African men who called themselves chiefs (community leaders) but who sold their own into unknown Transatlantic horrors. Their rapacious greed is continued today by a larger percentage of (un)modern African politicians, who simply continue centuries of continental plunder begun by the outsider.

The fact of a benign and gullible African involvement in the so-called trade has always been paraded by cynics who justify or deny the Black holocaust. They argue that slavery was already local to Africa before a combined nascent-capitalist European and a preceding 8th century Arabian invasion threw the continent into a millennial crisis and dehumanization. That crisis still resonates in other ways today—for example, in the guise of Africa's artificial economic, political, and social inequalities vis-à-vis the globe, which are engineered from without with the help of those African village-idiot politicians from within. These stupid critics conveniently forget the fact that slavery was a form of labour common to all societies in the world from classical Rome to 12th century Europe as well as to medieval Africa. In their sophistry they ignore the truth that original African slavery was of the relatively harmless domestic type to be differentiated from chattel slavery—the external (largely) European and (to a degree) Arabian variations, which tore the continent apart.

The point of emphasizing a rhetoric of the Stupid is that it is the loadstone that attracts that perennial dissimulation, which sustains the eternal ravaging of the continent from without and increasingly from within amongst its deadweight and corrupt sit-tight politicians and military dictators since independence in the late 1950s and early 1960s—this is apart from the lone example of South Africa, which only threw off the colonial yoke in 1994. All these internal and external players believe, like Adolf Hitler and one of his henchmen, Joseph Goebbels, that if you lie big and long enough, it will catch on and stick as truth. They trade in those illusions sold daily to African peoples. These tired folk, harassed forever from outside and inside, are still being inveigled and burdened with so many bogus wares—from foreign religion and language (beyond their practicalities) to unworkable foreign political and economic systems, all with the aim of sustaining the Stupidity that has been deployed to keep the continent's peoples chained down and held back by the greed of the larger world and a few internal collaborators. Such deceptions sometimes take on the semblance of truth, good intentions, or a general positive air. But it is usually the same old-school buffoonery presented as fine speech—like the occasional Western "Africa-rising" analyses and comments by Western 'experts' on Africa as represented by metropolitan newspapers, financial and otherwise, and allied think tanks. It is this latter pseudo-benevolent and, according to Chinua Achebe, "bleeding-heart" model of the Stupid which has now tragically consumed an embattled 'friend of Africa.'

He often dabbles in the absurd with a Beckettian flourish, as witnessed by his many previous Idiot commentaries. With an especially insane write-up in 2017 adjudicating for a re-colonization of Africa, Bruce Gilley dived into an already brackish and bottomless swimming pool of Stupid in which he has since been drowning. This supercilious political scientist professes Stupidity at Portland State University. As noted, it was not the first time he has made incendiary statements in the name of freedom of speech. His self-comportment is much like that of a drunken alcoholic who, suddenly remembering in his torpor that he possesses freedom of speech—in this case White privilege and misbehaviour—staggers up, goes on a verbal rampage and begins to embarrass his immediate family as well as the entire world by insulting any passers-by with frothy, epileptic speech let loose, while undressing and giddily dancing naked in public to a music in his own head.

Gilley's vituperations have been given enough sound bites and cyberspace bytes as well as enough ink impressions; they bear no repeating beyond the briefest summary. Gilley's Idiot recommendation to the right-wing is that the West should recolonize the continent of Africa—even at the invitation of Africans—because colonialism happened, and it was a good, good thing! The different levels and shades of Stupid inherent in this cringe-worthy and sick recommendation are so earth-shattering that for a so-called political scientist to even think of it is mind-boggling—unless of course he is a closet White supremacist and card-carrying member of the KKK, or a collaborator of that new-age and chic Alt-Right variety of Stupid.

Its myopia and historical insensitivity apart, any talk of resurrecting colonialism to 'save Africa' or formerly colonized Indigenous peoples as well as any yet uncolonized patch of the earth—inconceivable as that is—indirectly suggests that such peoples would be justified in amassing weapons of mass annihilation in anticipation. They would need it for self-preservation and self-defence from a yet unknown enemy. Gilley is unwittingly suggesting that, were Africa some tech-savvy Wakanda in the Middle Ages and had, say, advanced nuclear weapons, it would not have been enslaved or later colonized. He insinuates that the continent should prepare itself, even today, to acquire advanced weaponry for the purposes of self-defence from possible re-colonization, official or otherwise. After all, self-preservation has been the very secret rationale for recent or past proliferation amongst imperial, as well as belligerent or even peaceful, countries.

Self-preservation is the reason North Korea began to amass missiles; it is also the reason it, at some point, apparently stopped stockpiling; in other words, that country's goal of retaliatory military capability had been achieved. It was time for it to sit at the negotiation table, with a cruise missile smouldering in Kim Jung Un's back pocket. Gilley's poisonous write-up suggests that North Korean nuclear stockpiling and tests were, and will be, justified and should be emulated by the African continent and any other international group, which might remotely suspect the possibility of a return to bondage and servitude via re-colonization. He insinuates that those ISIL terrorists were right to rampage and kill and maim in response to an often-expressed fear of domination and colonization by the USA. Under the breath of his inane article, he seems to ironically whisper: "Can anyone imagine a South Africa that will now willingly succumb itself to that old demonic Apartheid?" Gilley's un-smart "viewpoint essay"—as his publisher, the equally guilty and ironically titled *Third World Quarterly,* stupidly calls it— sets the imagination on fire. What would happen should Canada, for example, decide to save the First Nation from itself and reopen residential schools all over the country with the excuse that some overlooked historical lessons still need to be taught by the said schools? Gilley's bad good intentions—reminiscent of an old, disgraced kind of 'progress' and spurred on by an equally jaded Manifest Destiny—is a recipe for a mutually assured global destruction. That is, indeed, a strong and dark dose of Stupid.

Charlie Hebdo's Ghost

Contemporary democratic ideals about freedom of expression are distilled into that metonymic and tired but valid catchall, "The pen is mightier than the sword." It is usually buried amongst other common aphorisms—buried, that is, but not forgotten. This is because flowers have grown over that 'grave' expression and yielded overgrown fruits. Some of the most round and constipated of them (for human rights violators) are the numerous PEN centres around the world or Amnesty International and Human Rights Watch. All are part of about eighty sundry rights-focused NGOs, which make up the umbrella group, International Freedom of Expression Exchange or IFEX.

The Cartoonists Rights Network International (CRNI) is of urgent concern here, even if only indirectly—by way of the Parisian cartoon publication, *Charlie Hebdo*. It is in support of that lively organ belonging to the body of CRNI that the American PEN centre suddenly finds itself in 'cartoonish' skirmishes in which individual writer-members disagree fiercely in public and throw large darts—oversized poisoned pens—at each other across different ideological streets. This is the ghost of the matter—because this situation resurrects the dozen dead French cartoonists cut down in a bitter hailstone of bullets by two 'Islamic' terrorist siblings on 7 January 2015.

It is in the mourning of human rights—twelve times felled—and in showing moral support for, and solidarity with, *Charlie Hebdo* that American PEN honours that publication during its annual Gala that same year. That organization performs its obligation and executes its mandate to protect freedom of expression and recognize

bravery, fatal and otherwise, and the expressing of the same wherever it appears. Why then does PEN's traditional salute to freedom
of expression become the occasion for a divided house? I think that
the problem has to do with a confusion arising out of the deployment
of the wrong language in describing the right phenomenon. This
is ironic for an organization whose membership consists mainly of
writers—Poets, Essayists and Novelists (PEN)—who happen, in this
instance, to have been defeated by language. Witness the argument
of a small but significant group of protesting American PEN writers:

> [o]ur concern is that, by bestowing the Toni and
> James C. Goodale Freedom of Expression Courage
> Award on Charlie Hebdo, PEN is not simply convey-
> ing support for freedom of expression, but also val-
> orizing selectively offensive material: material that
> intensifies the anti-Islamic, anti-Maghreb, anti-Arab
> sentiments already prevalent in the Western world.

The over-two-hundred signatories to that letter from which
the above excerpt is taken have a valid but problematic argument
against American PEN as a representative body and against *Charlie
Hebdo*, both of whom, in turn, equally have valid but questionable
opinions in this matter. Everyone is right and wrong at the same
time and simply talk past each other.

On the one hand, protesting American PEN writer-members
suggest, in the language of their letter, that *Charlie Hebdo* continues a French colonial ethos of demonizing the Other in a supposedly postcolonial and global world. On the other, the publication's
official position is that its caricatures are an "equal opportunity
offense," which neither discriminates between races nor cherry-
picks the personalities, institutions, or religion it mocks. *Charlie*

Hebdo insists on its right to satirize violence against personal opinion, no matter how distasteful. That is irrespective of whether that protest apparently negates and demonizes the 'Maghreb,' 'Islam,' or 'Arab.' However, the protesters ignore the fact that a very large population of world Muslims—some Asian, some African, and others European—are not Arabs nor do they live in, or identify with, the Maghreb. Of course, those substantives could stand in as metonymies for the entire Muslim world. But that would ignore the fact that identities are more and more fluid and complex in a global world and that a small crowd, no matter how loud, cannot represent the multifarious population of Muslims in the world—East-meets-West-meets-South and collides with the North.

In deploying a binary divisive 'we-them vs. you-you' language in their letter, the protesting PEN members unwittingly fall into the trap of a discredited clash of civilization rhetoric reminiscent of Samuel P. Huntington. And all of that because the Western relationship to Islam is mediated by a language that seems to have remained static since the Middle Ages when King Richard I (the Lion Heart) of England did battle with Muslim Saracens led by the Sultan Saladin during the Third Crusade. Basically, there is an urgent sociolinguistic and theological need to separate the word Muslim or 'Islam' from 'terrorism' because, by a spiritual equation, a Muslim cannot be a terrorist at the same time. That is irrespective of the fact that some self-proclaimed Muslims interpret the "sword verses" in the Al Quran literally and devoid of historical context for their own political goals—hence another unfortunate and confusing term, "political Islam." While religion and real politik can form a toxic and explosive mix, the spiritual is totally anti-political and not at all enamoured with the inordinate material desire for which 'political Islam' is a tool.

Cultic behaviour as an ill social force, its admixture with illicit power and the neurotic and its propensity for evil, ought to be re-appraised as 'corrupt religion.' There is a need to stop confusing gross religion with spirituality—whether of the Christian, Muslim, Hindu, or Buddhist variety. Inferior, empty, and ritualistic religion—in other words, the cult—is a confine within which some, or groups of, people in the 'lunatic fringe' hide and commit acts of terrorism, depravity, dark occultism, or demonic behaviour, all of which eschew the spiritual. Such individuals or groups should be seen for what they are: religious and psychic criminals and spiritual outlaws but certainly not Muslims—or Christians or Hindu. To conceive of that otherwise is to give these outlaws political legitimacy. Referring to terrorists as 'Muslims' aids them in their terrorism.

For example, the cultic American Pastor, Jim Jones, who perpetuated the "Guyana Tragedy" was definitely not a Christian but a cultic thug. That psychotic character murdered over 914, including 200 children, through cyanide poisoning under some mad delusion of a need for instant and collective rapture. He was never seen as a 'Christian terrorist' but as a sick criminal and leader of a cult. Nor was David Koresh, the loony cultic 'prophet' of the Branch Davidians sect seen as a 'Christian terrorist'; he was just a criminal exploiting the Christian religion. That some exploit Islam for dark deeds and declare that they act on behalf of Allah does not make them Muslims. And it does not matter how 'normal' or widespread such behaviour has become. We need new concepts and a new language for describing it. 'Muslim terrorist,' 'Islamic terrorist' or 'political Islam' are lazy concepts; collectively they are a confusing and imprecise oxymoron! This is because murder is against all esoteric laws within any religion. It is 'irreligion'—a deep and frightening ignorance of spiritual matters.

No one, perhaps, is better placed than Salman Rushdie to warn us about the dangers of misconstruing and misunderstanding the nature of terror. For his writing the novel, The *Satanic Verses*, a fatwa and bounty were placed on his head by a terrorist and cultic irreligious mullah posing as a Muslim. It is imperative to listen to an innocent man forced to hide from terror for many years. In this *Charlie Hebdo* affair, he insinuates the need for a distinction between religious criminals and hijackers of Islam in admonition to the protesting American PEN writers:

> [t]his issue has nothing to do with an oppressed and
> disadvantaged minority [Muslim]. It has everything
> to do with the battle against fanatical Islam, which
> is highly organised, well funded, and which seeks to
> terrify us all, Muslims as well as non Muslims, into a
> cowed silence.

'Fanatical Islam' is, again, a misconception here. Those terrorists simply hide behind the veil of Islam to commit crimes against humanity. This is why an American PEN award to *Charlie Hebdo* is justified and proper. What is not justified is to offer such an award as a reproach to 'Islamic terrorism,' in response to cartoons which also wrongly and sacrilegiously lampoon the prophet and Islam. Again, terror and Islam are not synonymous. It is the conflation of Islam with terrorism that discomfits everyone from political pundits to presidents or scholars and street-side philosophers when they try to approach the subject. That aporia immobilizes moral consensus and defeats the world of policy when it seeks to legislate against these criminals and social misfits.

And, while *Charlie Hebdo* appears to be right in satirizing the perceived institutional support for terrorist activity, namely Islam, its prophet, and other related icons, that magazine's action lies on the borders of hate speech—if not sacrilege—because of the same problem of definitions pervading the whole affair. All parties involved, including American PEN, are right and wrong at the same time in their different positions. What unites these actors is their failure to re-think the language with which Islam is discussed in the public sphere. This is a situation that further problematizes popular imaginations of the Islamic and colours political discussions and analyses about Islam, Muslims, and radicalism. Everyone seems to have developed a blind spot to the atrophy or inadequacies of the usual language of address where that religion is concerned. Is the terror group ISIS an Islamic group, for example? Definitely not; it is a band of criminals, which murders Christians as well as Muslims. Their excesses prove the point that Islam and terrorism have nothing in common.

The dissenting writer-members and their representative body, American PEN, have been deceived by language. They are both victims of the trickster Yoruba god, Esu, who sets two friends upon each other by sending a man to walk between them wearing a traditional cap, the *fila*, coloured totally white on one side and totally black on the other. Both friends see different sides of the same fila and therefore have different languages for describing the same phenomenon. One insists it is white and the other swears it is black. So do these two close friends engage in total battle and so begins the greatest enmity between bosom friends. In this wrong-headed PEN family quarrel, only the criminal terrorists have won. They must be laughing, re-energised for their next suicide mission! Is the PEN then mightier than the terrorist sword?

The Ree, the Roo, the Raa!; or
Bene Bene Pendentes!

It is surprising that the world was surprised at, or by, the little drama in The Church as one sitting Pope resigned and another ascended the throne of Peter. For waywardness, that event is insignificant compared to several papal commotions during the Middle Ages in Europe. Although it is a literary work, Geoffrey Chaucer's satirical *Canterbury Tales* (1475) is, in part, a useful sociological, —albeit fictionalised—account of medieval ethical and moral clerical excesses. One variant of that was the 'selling' of indulgences to believers. Professional 'pardoners' granted shrift in exchange for lucre. One of the colourful characters through whom Chaucer focalises his lampooning narrative is the satirical figure, 'The Pardoner.' In "The Pardoner's Tale" that protagonist mocks the clergy, whom he personifies, by declaring:

> If gifts your change of heart and mind reveal,
> You'll get my absolution while you kneel.
> Come forth, and kneel down here before, anon,
> And humbly you'll receive my full pardon;
> Or else receive a pardon as you wend,
> All new and fresh as every mile shall end,
> So that you offer me each time, anew,
> More gold and silver, all good coins and true.

Chaucer wrote of a time when faith was on its knees like a sinner or a shrunken beggar, a time when the steeple was as crooked as the tilting Tower of Pisa. This was the dark ages in clerical as well as in any other term: Popes fought for office like the nastiest of mafia bosses; devilish intrigue and executions were not exempted.

For example, the phenomenon now described as the Western Schism, consolidated between 1378 and 1417, was a situation in which an official Pope and one or two equally legitimate 'anti-Popes' existed simultaneously between Rome and Avignon, France. The height of such political brouhaha was 1409 when three Holinesses co-existed, installed one after the other by the same conclave of disgruntled cardinals in that one unholy instance. Across that era, the Holy See sees to it that wicked entertainment is provided to its admirers, secular and lay alike. But no histrionic compares to the catastrophe—for a very misogynist clergy—of accidentally installing a female Pope in Rome or Avignon in the 9th century.

If true, that is probably the first serious documented case of 'passing' in history—way ahead of its appearance in slave-owning America when bi- or multi-racial slaves who looked White enough simply passed for White and lived a more humane existence. Women in the medieval period were not much more than cattle—just like the Slavic people from whom the word 'slave' derives. And since poor nutrition and the shaven heads of priests, not to talk of cross-dressing amongst the clergy, bent the features of man or woman to a sexless blur, it was possible for the latter to pass by crossing genders and thus escaping slavish conditions towards upward social mobility. This is much within the same existential goals which made Slavs convert to Christianity because The Church declared that the Christian ideal precluded a follower of Christ from being a slave. Medieval gender and social transgressions provided the opportunity such that a certain John Anglicus who had no 'balls' could nevertheless become a man, a priest—and a Pope.

An embarrassed Church vigorously refutes the existence of Her Holiness, Popess Joan—La Papessa. She is myth or legend, the result of medieval protestant anti-church propaganda, and a figment of our modern imagination. All that, despite over five hundred ancient monastic chronicles of her existence and irrespective of evidence from pre-modern art, architecture, Church literature and the literature—a chapter of Giovanni Boccaccio's *Famous Women* (1374) focuses on her, myth or no myth. This mysterious lady Pope is an elephant in the room, visible and invisible all at once. Be that as it may. Perhaps she never actually existed. There is, however, an aspect of this legend that suggests otherwise.

The story concludes that Popess Joan was unmasked during a procession. She went into labour and gave birth in broad daylight, right under scandalised Roman noses. Since that ancient 'tragedy,' a checking of the candidate's phallic 'vitals' precedes every papal selection. He sits in a special tall chair cut out in the middle such that his balls might hang and are visible to observing cardinals, who walk by in a file. The ritual is completed with the conclave individually bearing witness and declaiming in Latin as it files past: "testiculos habet; et bene pendentes!"; meaning roughly, "testicles he has and they hang well!" Or simply in the vernacular, "he is well-hung!"

If that account is true, then there is no stronger proof of the existence of a distant female Pope than this clerical phallic annunciation. The shadow of that matriarch is so overpowering that she practically makes boys out of men, such that they must play with each other's balls and prove their maleness, *bene-bene-pendentes*. Ironically, the only serious proof of La Papessa's existence is that very act of her historical denial and erasure by a hysterical clergy. This is anxiously marked in time by the viewing of scrotums, the joyous declamations; by the pendulous swaying of testicles—

ree-roo-raa—blown by woman-harsh religious winds as they depend down from the high ritual chair; and, of course, by the jubilant erection rocking that chair in spiritual ecstasy and patriarchal triumph! At least no eunuch or woman is supposed to sit there. In short, the whole ceremony of papal installation since La Papessa is fixated on the phallus, swollen, aggressive, and misogynist. Why must this tiny bit of muscle have such dizzying sway—ree-roo-raa—over male clerical senses? The answer might be religio-psychosocial.

Christian iconography is replete with phallic symbols, the most immediately visible being the Church steeple, along with the not-so-obvious ubiquitous 'cross'—very much phallic in its original ancient Babylonian design and pagan sexualised intent. These two icons will suffice, although other near inexhaustible examples exist—especially of the textual, linguistic sort within a scripture almost entirely written by men, except for the book of Ruth. The result of ancient religious male chauvinism is this primitive clerical masculinist and Hobbesian arrogance in the 21st century, which excludes women—and persecutes children.

It is persecution for the child when that ungainly weight, the-ree-the-roo-the-raa of the swinging phallus, pulls many a holy man asunder and he crumbles before the image of a helpless altar boy. Only a detachment from that pendulous weight will provide any kind of stability for the body of Christ. And detachment can only come if the pulpit overcomes its original fear—a woman Pope. Until La Papessa returns, that bodily clock will continue to tick, sway and whirr—ree-roo-raa! Church and state will not know rest.

The Middle East is a Fiction

As cliché as it might sound or read that 'truth is sometimes stranger than fiction,' the series of persistent symbolic and literal political explosions in the Middle East and North Africa during the 2010 – 2012 Arab Spring, country after dazed country, proved that truism right once again.

'…First it was sunny Tunisia, next the jewel, Egypt; Jordan, Yemen and then Bahrain, Syria, inscrutable Libya, until the virus spreads across the hot desert and drove fear into the hearts of Princes, Sheiks, and benevolent dictators…' That preceding sentence could easily begin the epic narrative of the struggle between power and citizenship that the Middle East and North Africa became. Some of the greatest poets or storytellers from that region could easily have written that novel—Nawal El Sadawi, Mahmud Darwish, Yashar Kemal, Orhan Pamuk, or the younger Hisham Matar and Mohsin Hammid. But I will give precedence to the art of Nobel laureate Naguib Mahfouz, whose expansive powers are tailor-made to capture the erstwhile epic tale, beginning in Egyptian antiquity on the banks of the Nile and spanning the northern rims of Africa and the tiniest village on the farthest reach of the dessert.

Mahfouz; because his literary breadth and love of the sublime was obvious in his seminal ambitious plan to write a series of thirty interrelated books—all stories that were to capture the entire sweep of Egyptian history from the time of pharaohs. He only succeeded in giving us three of them—*Mockery of the Fates* (1939), *Rhadopis* (1943), and *The Struggle of Thebes* (1944)—before the social and political ferment and urgency of the Egyptian moment dictated that

73

he emphasises the living present. He then gave us the monumental Cairo Trilogy of about one thousand and five hundred pages: tale after tale, his vision, social conscience, anti-establishment politics, activism, and expansive literary range make him the perfect would-be chronicler of the sublime fiction of an 'impossible' Arab Spring.

However, the future he envisioned but failed to write was unfolding. I can feel Mahfouz, great socialist and symbol of modern Arab enlightenment, rattle his coffin, realising that life has tricked him; his great tale was being written by a truth that is stranger than any fiction he could have dreamed up: a single personal story in the life of an ordinary man triggers an extraordinary revolution across a whole subcontinent. In Tunisia, Mohamed Bouazizi became, according to Elizabeth Day in the London Observer of 15th May, 2011, "the drop that tipped over the vase" in the Middle East. Nevertheless, and beyond the main facts of the precipitating encounter between a symbol of corrupt officialdom and our Mahfouzian protagonist, Day emphasises that the ongoing revolution was based on a lie—the lie that the revolution was preceded by a slap.

As far as truths go, we could draw on José Eduardo Agualusa's character, the surrogate father in *My Father's Wives* who finally breaks the news of his adult daughter, Laurentina's, true paternity with the rhetorical defence: "How many truths make up a lie?" The surrogate father, according to Jennie Erdal in the *London Guardian* of 20th December 2008, "defends his lie on the grounds that it contained many truths, all of them happy." How 'happy' is the lie that on December 17, 2010, an official of a corrupt and repressive Tunisian State dared to deliver the "slap that sparked a revolution," as Day puts it? Fedia Hamdi is a woman in a fiercely patriarchal Islamic world. How could she have hit a Moslem man in the face as she policed his public fruit and vegetable cart or stall? Due to the 'insult,' amongst other outrages, the street vendor, Bouazizi, took a bath in that stupendous source of Arab wealth—gasoline—and lit himself up as if in purification.

While the bare facts were as real as the eyes could see, the embellishments were so fictitiously overwhelming that the truth of the actual events was eclipsed in the memory of Bouazizi's mother who, when asked to recount what kind of man her son was, replied: "I can't think of one single memory." Except, perhaps, that 'he set himself on fire because a 'mere' woman slapped him'? We choose what truths to believe or are conditioned to believe the 'truthful lie,' and vice-versa. Hamdi, who was scapegoated and jailed by Tunisian officialdom for being the 'reason' for the storm in the Middle Eastern cauldron—not just a teacup—has consistently denied slapping an Arab man! Nevertheless, so overwhelming was this one happy lie that it erased the facts and became an important narrative in the reality of a new Arab dawn.

Importantly, an indignant Bouazizi sets not only himself but also all of Arabia on fire—not necessarily due to that 'impossible' slap but because of the accustomed official injustices that the fiction emphasises. Hamdi is not just a woman but also a policewoman. Bad enough when official brutality wears a turban, but it becomes an intolerable nightmare when a Hijab frames it. The region bursts into flames of protest against millennial official oppression, unfreedom, corruption, unemployment, and dispossession. These are the social injustices Mahfouz wrote about and against. The street is demanding some of what he preached—the attendant democratising and liberal advocacy in his work, which caused militants to attack him with knife stabs to the neck in 1994 at age 82.

Even if the truth 'lies' in the grave with Bouazizi—the myth of the slap was his rumoured claim—the lie is still 'happy' enough; that is, the lie is 'truthful' enough, to have resulted in a seismic shift in the popular emotion of the Arab world and its relationship to official Islamic power. The means justifies the desired ends—at one remove. At one remove because on the other end of a 'realistic' scale, the sort of revolution going on is totally unimaginable except in the realm of a Malfouzian narrative—but it is at the same time possible because only narrative makes anything possible.

The moral is that it is 'narrative' which creates an objective world that we then invest with 'reality,' with meaning; that the reality we construct rules our lives, sinks into the unconscious and settles heavily with the force of 'divine' truth. The objective world mirrors fiction because our realities are moulded by the stories we tell ourselves and invest with 'truth'—as Laurentina's surrogate father does in Agualusa's story. It is not for nothing that fiction is believable, that we suspend disbelief while watching a movie or a play, while reading a story—because if you can imagine it, then it is possible, so to speak. In short, we create and negotiate reality. This is because, as opposed to those mimetic theories which insist that fiction mirrors the objective world, sometimes the objective world mimics fiction. This is particularly so when, and since, our reality is a human construction that has no solidity in any 'real' world 'out there'—if we are willing to suspend the fiction of the 'divine' or 'natural' for a minute.

In Arabia, the man in the street has broken his shackles, which were welded together in the smithy of the stories he has been told—religious stories, myths of origins, and nationalisms—stories of the infallible and benevolent cult figure of the leader—next-of-kin to 'God,' in whose name the latter demands, commands, and indeed wills a blind, iron allegiance to a repressive Islamic state. In sitcom-like moments, besieged political leader after leader told and still tell alternative stories, selling fictions, rewriting events in contradiction to global public knowledge of facts. Saif Al-Islam, Muammar Gaddafi's son and official megaphone, was a more consummate spinner of tales than anyone else. He was like the Black albino in Agualusa's *The Book of Chameleons*, "whose profession it is to invent 'better pasts' for Angola's new elite."

Saif Al-Islam invents 'better pasts' with Gaddafian truculence to legitimise his dynasty's inordinate desire to hold onto power. He insults the intelligence of the global public in proclaiming like 'God' that "there is no problem," "the people of Libya are happy with their leader", "there are no riots or disaffection." To do this he inhabited an in-between world of mirrors. He lost himself in his own fictional and imaginary world and became delusional—much like a cartoon figure as he lied away copiously on the cable TV screen, mouthing words that had no referent of meaning in the face of riots, albeit officially denied, which raged on Libyan streets, and finally led to a civil war in that country. Lies, when told often enough, becomes true. Every propagandist knows this. In Erdgal's review of Agualusa's *The Books of Chameleons*, "[o]ne character [...]—a novelist—when pressed to say whether he writes lies deliberately or out of ignorance, declares that he is a liar by vocation, indeed he lies with joy. Fictions, so we are to understand, are uniquely suited to getting at truths." While that might be true for didactic purposes, it is also clear that the stories we tell ourselves create our daily reality.

It is well known that Mahfouz was branded an apostate by the Islamic right. He was hounded in late life, threatened, and attacked viciously. But he is getting his revenge. In the scriptural novel— much like *Children of Gebelawi*—which Mahfouz wrote from the grave and which was then filming in the Middle East, he irritated the religious right. In his sublime fashion, he set out to fictionalise the Bible, the Al Quran, the Bhagavad-Gita or the Srimad Bhagavatam, the Mahabharata, and so on. As preface he poses the disclaimer: 'These are works of fiction. All names, places, characters, and incidents are a product of the author's imagination. This is why... first it was sunny Tunisia, next the jewel, Egypt;...' Mahfouz writes like this to let us know that his fictionalisation of the scriptures is not fiction precisely because it is fiction. We are (not) free to believe what we want. The streets of Syria, Jordan, Bahrain, Libya, Saudi Arabia etc. proved him right. They now believe other stories.

'Easing' the Arab Spring

Naming of Parts" is Henry Reed's long poem about the Second World War and the first of five related sections in his 1942 collection, *The Lessons of War*. In the narrative poem under focus, a drill sergeant instructs recruits in the use of simple weaponry in a matter-of-fact and conversational tone:

> This is the lower sling swivel. And this
> Is the upper sling swivel, whose use you will see,
> When you are given your slings. And this is the
> piling swivel,
> Which in your case you have not got…

A second voice—the distracted thoughts of a recruit who is also a poet—mentally echoes the clipped military speech of the first speaker. The calm and conversational tone of the sergeant is matched or even surpassed by the meditative ambulatory ruminations of the daydreaming soldier-poet in a repetitive echo. He transforms the prosaic, colloquial thoughts of the drillmaster into impassioned poetry. The one's running commentary and monologue is married to the other's poignant observations about the sublime spring environment, which fires the poet-recruit's wandering imagination:

> Today we have naming of parts. Yesterday,
> We had daily cleaning. And tomorrow morning,
> We shall have what to do after firing. But today,
> Today we have naming of parts. Japonica
> Glistens like coral in all of the neighboring gardens,
> > And today we have naming of parts.

The poet denotes the brilliance and bloom of spring as counter-points to the drill sergeant's mechanical and toneless chatter about the cold brutality of guns and their deadly functions. The ensuing parallelism and contrast casts a shimmering glow over the whole, has a defamiliarising effect, expands the field of signification, and imbues us with a sense of the overwhelming beauty of spring, and life—even in the tragic situation of impending war. That is just one out of the many guarded ironies in this lyric.

Henry Reed's classic poem on soldiering is apt in thinking about Bashar al-Assad, Syria, and the Arab Spring. Al-Assad is like Reed's soldier poet-persona, if only in the sense that both give military instructions; the one, towards the training of recruits in a World War II setting and the other, towards invading his own people in peacetime. The contrast does not end there. While the second protagonist in the poem under discussion is a recruit with a poet's sensibilities, al-Assad is a politician with a psychopathic killer's instincts. The distinctions are that Reed's soldier prepares recruits for a desperate and necessary Second World War campaign, while al-Assad, the mindless politician and egomaniac, directs his murderous troops to unleash mayhem under no threat from a Hitler.

Irony is an overriding but silent rhetorical strategy in the"Naming of Parts" and in al-Assad's massacre of his own people and the toothless global political response to it. Unchecked, al-Assad, the experienced political gamer and predator—with his own people as game—is forever arrogant and ignores the moral of militarily preparing inexperienced recruits in the "Naming of Parts." 'Easing' the spring of a gun can shatter the beauty of spring, the season. Guns should be discharged only when necessary: in the heat of battle against marauding enemies, not in the decimation of protesting civilians. The last is precisely what al-Assad does—murder those civilians who he is supposed to be protecting as leader of Syria. Understandably, he is no statesman but a thug, and his acts equal a 'civicide.'

And the United Nations, established in 1945 towards global peace and stability, is itself too troubled internally to enforce real and sustainable peace in Syria. Due to a "politics of the belly" amongst UN member states, particularly China and Russia, the NATO-led military solution to Muammar Gaddafi's USA-alleged but unproven 'civicide' in Libya is not applicable in Syria. As such, al-Assad, the sad man and sadist of the Arab Spring, becomes a modern-day *Australopithecus africanus*, a killer ape wielding a murderous club. That gangling, ungainly, and "unfeathered two-legged thing," as John Dryden would have it, continues to maim and to kill. This is why the opposition is forced to fight a losing and undignified battle. And they seem to be listening to the voice of our drillmaster in *Lessons of the War*:

> Things may be the same again; and we must fight
> Not in the hope of winning but rather of keeping
> Something alive: so that when we meet our end,
> It may be said that we tackled wherever we could,
> That battle-fit we lived, and though defeated,
> Not without glory fought.

As the shadows of a spring day and the dreadful monotone lengthen, some of the rather oblivious recruits in *Lessons of the War*, mere boys—coming to a realisation of the terror ahead of them—begin to snivel or weep as they listen to the dispassionate frank and terrible voice of the drill sergeant. The sergeant, agent of death, bemoans their weakness:

I have no wish to be inconsiderate,
But I see there are two of you now, commencing to
snivel.
I do not know where such emotional privates can
come from.
      Try to behave like men.

Nevertheless, the recruits, overwhelmed as it were by the beauty of life around them as "[o]n the fields of summer the sun and the shadows bestow/[v]estments of purple and gold," mourn their own pending deaths. Many of them will probably never see another spring day after their first campaign. Syria mourns its dead and dying every day while the UN gives al-Assad reprieve because "there may be dead ground in between" diplomacy and the UN's military will.

One of the 'lessons of the war' is that these recruits, who have yet to fire a bullet or see an enemy formation, are already casualties. And so is every Syrian on the battlefront or in some quiet peaceful corner of the earth—because for the "far removed there is wailing." For every fallen Syrian in Damascus there are tears to be reaped in Dachau. "The casualties are not those who are dead/They are well out of it," according to another poet, John Pepper-Clarke, writing about another civil war. Those recruits are being prepared to die and mourn their own deaths even before they have seen an enemy gunner. War, an unpleasant business, is described by the drillmaster in the most pleasant and calmest of tones, just as the UN plays 'numbers' with Syrian lives. And the prospect of Henry Reed's recruits killing and being killed becomes therefore even more frightening—especially against the background of a bright spring day with flowers blooming all over the earth. The 'lessons of the war' are that 'you will not survive it,' the title of the poetry collection seems to suggest. The weight of irony invokes tears in the recruits. Never to see all this spring beauty again! And to be sold death in this cheap way of naming it chivalry. This is also the tragedy of Syria. Death presented as chivalry: that is what the UN does when it prevaricates.

Al-Assad and the UN do not allow an 'easing' of the Arab spring, a releasing of the romantic promises of a full-blown democratic promise in a revolution which began with Mohammed Bouazzi's self-immolation in Tunisia, inflaming the whole region, but which is still inconclusive—in Egypt, Bahrain, Yemen, Tunisia, Lybia, and so on. But Syria alone clearly epitomises the indecisions of the Arab Spring. Al-Assad is a conscienceless, unromantic criminal (masquerading as leader) under the unwritten moral laws that guide the soldier-poet, who tries to capture the terror of the moment in the beauty of spring:

> And this you can see is the bolt. The purpose of this
> Is to open the breech, as you see. We can slide it
> Rapidly backwards and forwards: we call this
> Easing the spring. And rapidly backwards and forwards
> The early bees are assaulting and fumbling the flowers:
> They call it easing the Spring.

The bees bring in the spring season as they flirt with flowers. Syria's spring is trapped in a wintry war and the fading of a hoped-for democracy. And the UN's diplomatic efforts resemble that of a bumblebee cavorting amongst a dazed Syrian citizenry. That August body appears more and more confused and helpless in May. And all is to no avail because "things only seem to be things" as the world fails Syria daily, a dictator sits in Damascus, and we cannot ease in the Arab Spring.

84

Sirens Knuckles Boots!

A South African Miners' strike in 2012 and that country's over-policing of it momentarily distracted the global public from the prevalent political Islam's sporadic baying at the moon. The shocking police lunacy was already a bad enough scene from the script of a classic Apartheid disaster like Sharpeville or Soweto. Only, there was a macabre twist. It was not the accustomed short-gun-toting White Apartheid police squad that is now carrying out target practice by aiming live ammunition at the fleeing backs of Black South African schoolchildren. Rather, it was mostly Black policemen in a Black ANC-ruled South Africa who gunned down forty-four protesting Black miners in a hail (Mary) of bullets.

True, some of the protesters wielded 'machetes and sticks'; true, it was rumoured that one even brandished a gun. Nevertheless, the riot police are a paramilitary force trained or 'supposedly' trained to disarm, disband, and scatter—and if the situation comes to a head, 'equipped' to give good tackle without breaking too much sweat or killing anyone. The riotous crowd of miners, as a disorderly uncoordinated body, simply represented the usual professional hazard. The South African police failed as a security force on all fronts—professionally, ethically, and as a member of the community.

More worrisome was the fact that this event resurrected the ghosts of many a brutalised, tortured, bloodied, and battered anti-Apartheid protester or activist—often Black, like Steve Biko, and sometimes White—on the long road to freedom. They were those who were forced to live on the edge of ruin, whose brave lives were ruled by the whip's razored swoosh, whose final stares, through glazed murdered eyes, were surprised in death by hot government-issued apartheid bullets—as if they only braced for the fall of the sjambok or a White-booted foot stomping down hard on a clenched and prostrate Black face. One should not even try to count the number of Black homesteads—the harmless children and their mothers—over whom the Apartheid juggernaut rolled on the streets and who were crushed to death; and the innumerable men and women harassed and driven insane by alienating exile or excruciating incarceration and pushed to suicide as the last refuge from their nightmares.

Interestingly, a government minister initially accused some of the miners of being indirectly responsible for the murders by dint of their association (as 'accomplices' in a strike) with the massacred. As if in anticipation of such a turn of events, online videos emerged, reflecting the miners' dazed, eloquent dying eyes staring in unbelief at an upended world from the dust where they writhe and plead without words: "poor wordless body in its fumbling ways," says Dennis Brutus. Perhaps a good thing he is not alive to witness this return to a system he (along with countless others) sacrificed all his life to end, especially when a minister performed an Apartheid-style (il)legal transference of criminal responsibility from bad government unto the citizen-victim, justifying that mass execution with the typical inhuman and evil logic of Apartheid. Conveniently, she, Ms. Minister, had a short memory of those injustices, which generations of South Africans had to valiantly fight against—at great costs—in order for her, a Black woman, to become cabinet minister in a 'free' South Africa. Zuma's 'threat' to investigate the matter was empty. It seems as if he planned to turn a blind eye to the police and their Apartheid-style crime and focus on the 'untouchable' multinational operators of the mines, whom his government is in bed with anyhow.

The dance macabre turned out to be a tacit official condoning of Apartheid-style state violence against the working poor. And precisely because of the staggering amount of platinum wealth, measured in billions of dollars, which they dig up from the caverns of the earth, the miners' impoverishment is a symptom of the dispossession of the Black working class by the transnational corporation—Lonmin and its ilk in this case—in collusion, surprisingly, with a comprador post-Apartheid ANC government. All that, despite the utopia symbolized in the optimism of Sam, that Black servant in Nadine Gordimer's *July's People*, who has to 'host' his unjustly impoverished, homeless, and penniless former overlords in a sudden extreme reversal of roles and fortunes within a simulated free South Africa. In reality, when over three hundred years of a Leviathan status quo had been overtaken by actual radical political change, no one could have expected the ongoing 21st century retrogression into Apartheid-era legal, civic, and socio-economic dispossession. This is why we are forced to step back in time and find ourselves in, for example, Malay Camp in 1942.

In the novel, *Mine Boy*, Xuma arrives in a mining ghetto town and siding called Malay Camp looking for work in the mines. It is a 'camp' because it is a mining settlement—poor, desolate, drunken, and brawling. It is not a place for the weak. The men, miners all, live their lives in the belly of the earth and most times come up gasping for air, coughing and dying. It is of course the Apartheid era, with the indigenous Black South African banished to the prison of townships, plagued by a life of official regimentation, harassed, policed, over-taxed, deprived of all economic- or self-advancement through education, and, for amusement, abandoned to liver-eroding, illicit and groggy evenings in that devil's watering hole called the shebeen. Their lives, like that of Daddy the drunk, dissolve in drink. That is the picture of the South African future, which Peter

Abrahams painted in *Mine Boy* in 1942. It is the future because the past—for example, 1942—was constructed as the hell it was in large part because of the gold deposits and 'rush,' which attracted the Boer and protracted colonial activity. Mines still physically dot the landmass of the country and seem to be a permanent feature of South Africa's socio-economic and political landscape. The future is always a present.

That future is at no time more present than right now everywhere as much as in contemporary South Africa, bedevilled by a plethora of social ills, including anti-Black xenophobia against other Black people from the continent—irrespective of their herculean external moral and financial supportive roles in bringing down Apartheid as a system. In the Malay Camp Black township ghetto of 1942, the evidence of a 'normal' and decent life is telegraphed to its wretched inhabitants only as a 'hum' from the 'city'—faint, distant, but deep; a persistent and humiliating thrill in the head of the poor. It is a White-only kind of noise inhabited by the powerful—those gods for whom Blacks or Indians were only kaffirs, wogs, and servants. Today, that hum is peopled by a different hue—Black. The Black South African elite has taken over those habitations where Whites were once gods. In other words, the current Black ruling class has maintained the White class and social hierarchies, along with their artificial conditions, which were installed by Apartheid. What has changed in South Africa is only the baton of power. Apartheid injustice, dispossession, and brutalities persist on both sides. Initially, power changed hands in 1994 to hope and promise, but the hand that now rules still carries the same clenched fist of the Apartheid years.

Yes, there is a minority, both Black and White, which enjoys the largess and goodies of freedom, but it is a very small minority indeed. South Africans—'the people,' White, Black, Indian or Jew, still exist under the sirens, the hard knuckles and jackboots of Apartheid conditions. In this ironic and cruel social and economic stasis, it is not only the people, the oppressed miners in this instance, who are 'mine boys.' It is not for nothing that Peter Abrahams' rebellious and fighting mine boy, 'Xuma,' of 1942 has been transformed into a contemporary 'Zuma,' former president of the republic of South Africa. While he competed with the erstwhile colonial master in pomp, pageantry, pleasure, and philandering within the colonial mansion, Zuma forgot his alter ego, Xuma, slaving thousands of miles under the earth in the mines of 1942; he forgot that his past and his future ought to find a political resolution in the present.

The multinational mining corporation, with all its rapacious digging, will eventually create a deep enough bottomless pit under the presidential mansion. And when the house eventually goes into a free fall, even before it hits a non-existent bottom, the ghost of Xuma, the activist, will have melted into ether, into a time past all other Zuma-s's sudden harsh 'deep' reality; and a future beyond approach for these Zuma-s, trapped as they will then be under a collapsed country. Jacob Zuma, symbol of all that is wrong with the ANC, was the original mine boy—that type that will go back into a collapsing mine if only just to please the master; he was furiously digging his way back into the earth, already burrowed deeper than a cricket.

World without End

End-time predictions have become an industry. The often-in-voked Mayan example is only a variation of a millennial disease. There exists a long, demented line of prophets, teachers, gurus, visionaries, clairvoyants, and 'wisemen' or plain con artists who all equally have the jobless ears of an impassive God. So, they invoke and are awarded apocalyptic contracts of floods, earthquakes, nuclear meltdowns, and rivers of liquid fire till the sky implodes and earth caves in. We are then either 'raptured' into heaven or we rupture here in a hell-on-earth—if left behind.

Of all the violent agitations for an end-of-the-world, the Pentecostal version is one of the most frightening. One reason is that it reads the Christian scripture literally, missing the deep metaphysical import of an esoteric-cum-philosophical book, and apportions celestial origins to a material—even if inspired—object. Another reason is that the sellers of nightmares rate their poisonous wares higher than any competing delusion. I am thinking of rival myopia found amongst another lunatic fringe, who equally believes in a physical heaven. But in this case, it is a cosmic realm with alluring virgins waiting to satisfy the suicide bomber's holy lust as recompense for his having criminally detonated innocent lives here on earth.

Those competing delusions derive from a lack of spiritual or metaphysical knowledge and sheer ignorance. They are based on the confusing of an abstract, imaginary realm with an impossibly physical, palpable, and solid existence. This is just the proof and symptom of a face-value understanding of those books that ought to be read esoterically rather than as literal magical texts. Or how else do we explain the inscrutable and 'rapturous' Harold Camping, one of the main protagonists of the American Bible belt? He has severally predicted the end of the world and publicly gone to extremes to prepare himself and his flock of sheep, over whose collective eyes he managed to repeatedly pull the wool. After each failed prediction he diminished into himself like a collapsed camping chair–one that folds into itself until it barely resembles a chair at all—and enters a deep, embarrassed silence for a while; only to erupt like a persistent boil on the skin of yet another time, another cursed prediction, another impending apocalypse.

We find the exaggerated instance of an already hyperbolic misreading of scriptures in the example of that expatriate American pastor from hell, Jim Jones of Jonestown, Guyana. This megalomaniac assumed the aspect of God and made up his mind that the world must end on November 18, 1978. But like Dylan Thomas's poet persona, he would "not go gently into that good night… [His young] old age would burn and rage at the close of day." He took 914 lives, 200 of them children, by legislating mass suicide through cyanide poisoning. And his 'Peoples Temple' drank till "the mug slipped from grip." Does the Bible itself not philosophise: "world without end"? That proposition is repeated in the old and new testaments of the King James Version—in Ephesians 3:21 and in Isaiah 45:17. While, and because, they read the "second coming" literally, doomsayers are forced to wax lyrical when confronted with simple, plain prose: "world without end." Those who go 'Camping' with the hysterical and neurotic probably do so because of the usual fear of death—even though it is a natural enough transition—and because of the silence and darkness that follows. Hence the Pentecostal insistence that life will go on after death in the usual earthly manner we experience daily, in the same physical body after resurrection, with a plethora of the ills and emotions that wrack that imperfect body, and with our usual worries, woes, and earthly desires. Our suicide bomber is in for a shock when he transitions from a palpable three-dimensional world of length, breadth and solid into a transparent, paper-thin ghostly two dimension—because "once you are dead you are dead." That is the un-Christian but level-headed re-thought of that long-suffering cuckold and most persecuted Jew and therefore cynical of fictional characters, James Joyce's Leopold Bloom in *Ulysses*.

Ulysses is unusually obsessed with questions of death and dying and the hereafter or lack thereof. Like Teju Cole's recent *Open City*—and though not as obvious—it is a 'walking' novel in which the protagonist traverses a city—in this instance, Dublin—in one day. Bloom's character alludes to Odysseus, and the former's journey through the city mimics the epic wanderings of the latter in Homer's *The Odyssey*. In the dark, funereal Hades chapter of that novel, Bloom marches to the cemetery with a funeral cortege during Paddy Dignam's burial. In the stream-of-thought style made famous by Joyce, this maverick, apostate Jew-turned-Catholic unbeliever ridicules the idea of a physical hereafter typical of the usual way Christians misread the Bible:

> Lots of them [the dead at the cemetery] lying around
> here: lungs, hearts, livers, old rusty pumps: damn the
> thing else. The resurrection and the life. Once you
> are dead you are dead. That last day idea. Knocking
> them all up out of their graves. Come forth, Lazarus!
> And he came fifth and lost the job. Get up! Last Day!
> Then every fellow mousing around for his liver and his
> lights and the rest of his traps. Find damn all of him-
> self that morning. Pennyweight of powder in a skull.
> Twelve grammes one pennyweight. Troy measure.

The ridiculousness of the raw physical sense in which Christians talk about the afterlife is expressed deprecatingly in the stream of Bloom's consciousness above.

What Joyce is saying through the thoughts of Bloom is that there is no proof of an afterlife in the usual Christian way it is described by the clergy and accepted by the laity. Beyond the physical world there are metaphysical, as opposed to physical, principles at work, which the church fathers refuse to comprehend. When one dies, the physical world has ended in a sense. Whatever comes after, if at all, is either beyond our comprehension or of a completely different order—a hyperreal or surreal and dreamlike state and so on. Hence 'once you're dead you are dead.' This is why another modernist, T.S. Eliot, like Joyce declares, "In my beginning is my end." The End begins at the moment of birth. In a Wole Soyinka poem, "Abiku," about death and reincarnation, the new-born 'abiku' child, whose mythical fate it is to be born and to die repeatedly in infancy is described as "shaping mounds [graves or death] from the yolk [of infancy or life]."

Every time another prophet of doom stands up in public to sell us his or her nightmares, we should be prompt in reminding him or her that the whole idea of an ending of the world is philosophically contradictory since the world ends every day for the departed. If they persist then we ought to sing them their own "Endsongs" as offered by the Nigerian poet, Chiedu Ezeanah:

> You have lost the world
> You've lost the words
> You reap plots of silence
> As silences dismantles the leaves
> As silences dismantles lives around me
> In the minute and hour approaching stars
> The trees stink of rain.

World without end, Amen.

The Example of Mandela

I come to bury Caesar, not to praise him..." So proceeds Mark Anthony's famous funeral oration in honour of Shakespeare's Julius Caesar, who has just succumbed to a bloody palace coup. The speech is also a backhanded slap at the guilty conspirators, Caius Cassius and the brutish Marcus Brutus—both "honourable men" who, despite being politically ambitious regicides in this matter, ironically justify their murderous act by accusing the deceased of diseased ambition.

Although, unlike the fictional Caesar, Nelson Mandela escaped the political assassin's dagger at the end and peacefully faded away in his sleep, his demise also inspired valediction as well as veiled malediction when his immortality is set against the corpses of those, at the time, living and mostly sit-tight, corrupt, or inept African leaders like Zimbabwe's Robert Mugabe or Nigeria's Sanni Abacha, who have the vision of maggots. That valedictory speech was given by a real-life orator with skills equal to that of a Mark Anthony— no less a skilled public speaker than American president, Barack Obama. He gave, "measure for measure," a high-tension Shakespearian delivery with all the appropriate crowd-cues and all the necessary rhetorical flourishes compared to Anthony's.

However, a down-to-earth Mandela would, of course, eschew comparison to mighty, even if fictional, Caesar. But it must be said that he always displayed a political wisdom and regal carriage traceable to the dignity of his ancient African royal line. His post-Apartheid 'inhuman' embrace of otherwise sworn Apartheid-loving political enemies is regal, if not entirely godlike. Mandela's 'inhumanity' humanizes him to divine proportions. It is this supreme irony that is of interest here. How could a man named 'trouble' forgive his jailer, his tormentors, and centuries of Apartheid brutality without bitterness? This, certainly, is not human.

I virtually witnessed and still remember the convening of South Africa's unique Truth and Reconciliation Commission (TRC) with bemusement. This was, as the world knows, after Mandela's release from twenty-seven years of political prison and his ascension to his country's presidency. He had lost his prime behind bars, was estranged from family, did not see his children take their first tottering steps or lose their first set of teeth to the tooth fairy; nevertheless, he came out into the staggering light of freedom to leave the darkness behind him forever. He called for a truce and set up the psychological safety valve that was the TRC. He did not shout, 'give me my shorts, I want to riot!'

Without the TRC, the trauma, injustice, and hurt of the Apartheid years would surely have burnt the new South Africa to the ground. While the transition to democracy has not been without some post-Apartheid hiccups, the TRC installed restorative justice through confession, contrition, and a reciprocal forgiveness, and mid-wifed democracy in South Africa. This was all possible due to the ancient African philosophy of Ubuntu embraced by Mandela as an African elder leader of the community. The African spirit of community required reconciliation and understanding preceded by penitence, as respectively tough and shaming as it was to demand the former of victims and the latter from perpetrators. Compromise, fellow feeling, and reconciliation are germane to the age-old village-square domestic and communal conflict-resolution style typical to the African continent before Euro-modernity.

Mandela's life re-enacts the example of a need for acknowledging our common humanity as preached by such heroic figures before him, like Mahatma Gandhi or Martin Luther King Jr. and other kindred spirits. It is testament to his wisdom and thoughtfulness that a man whose public and private life was mostly troubled—and whose middle name, Rolihlahla, colloquially means 'troublemaker'—should urge humanity to embrace peace by the example of his own selflessness, non-racial politics, and material sacrifices.

Oh, Canada!

Experience, Inexperience, and (Un)Canadian Poetics

The world system has relied on immigrants for its self-regeneration ever since Homo erectus first moved away from the horn of Africa to Eurasia through the Levantine corridor about 1.8 million years ago. Individuals or groups migrate in pursuit of an idea, a dream—or even nightmares. The fleet-footed "traverse" the earth, "exploring all her wide-flung parts with zest" like Dennis Brutus's romantic troubadour and "probing in motion sweeter far than rest/ her secret thickets with an amorous hand."

Usually, the kind of traveller in question arrives loaded down with expectation and energy, trailed by dust and spiced experiences from other places—for whatever they are worth; experiences that could flow into host economies and replenish or give them a boost. This is why it is bewildering that Canadian policymakers are slow to harness, assimilate, or localise immigrant energy and creativity and insist that, on entering Canada, immigrants should slough off their foreign experiences as a snake sheds its skin. To function effectively, the arriviste is told in business and social circles that he or she requires this nebulous descriptive referred to as 'Canadian experience.' Immigrants are denuded of their previous skills and infantilized as being inexperienced on arrival. They become tabula rasa—dumb-numb, unintelligent, and unintelligible walking curiosities. This is the point where the wayfarer's dream becomes a nightmare for many years after landing. He or she is either unemployed, under-employed, or completely blind-sided by being kidnapped into other pre-occupations at odds with initial education, training, and skills, which are usually acquired at a very high level.

A certain result of the deprecation of international experience construed as 'Canadian inexperience' is the loss of international expertise due to an irrational insistence on a Canadian experience that is unavailable at the point of entry. Stories abound of immigrant specialists like surgeons, teachers, accountants, and editors being forced, in a desperate bid to earn a living, into occupations beneath their skill levels and outside and below their areas of expertise. A consequence is the irony that an immigration system specifically designed to attract the highly skilled into a knowledge economy inadvertently encourages an erosion of knowledge. Immigration becomes a revolving door through which knowledge enters and exits almost immediately. This is nothing other than reverse immigration. It is a situation in which demographic gains in immigration numbers and added skills are lost due to their not being infused into the economic system or because people are forced to return to their countries of origin or immigrate further. Those who stay behind because they are 'trapped' are like tolerated guests at a citizenship party—good for numbers but faceless, voiceless, emasculated and, more significantly, economically unproductive. As a matter of fact, and as a first in Canada, the Ontario Human Rights Commission has recently couched such exclusions in terms of a violation of the rights of new Canadians to economic agency. What also needs to be articulated are the immigration losses to Canada's socio-economic utility.

Reverse immigration is a knife that cuts both ways, and the bleeding is thick and visible on both sides. Those settlers—doctors, lawyers, teachers, accountants, pilots, and so on—whose foreign training and professional experiences are negated by an unofficial but ubiquitous statute of exclusion called Canadian experience, cannot, in turn, bring their creativity, skills, and vision to bear on the building of a young nation that actually requires urgent and regular renewals in numbers and in the trades, the professions, and businesses. It is a matter of fact that due to falling birth rates, increased life expectancies, and lower mortality, Canada and most Western democracies including the USA—and even Eastern Europe and Russia—have ageing populations. "Global aging" or, more accurately, an aging of the 'Western hemisphere,' is captured by several demographic descriptors such as "the greying of Europe," "The Silver Tsunami," or "Baby Bust" as compared to "Baby Boom," and so on.

An equivalent expression to capture economic aging specific to Canada alone ought to be referred to as "Canadian Experience" because that phrase is synonymous with and leads to all the negative socio-economic attributes and results of global aging. Moreover, a large demographic of Canada's meagre 38-million-strong population who possess Canadian experience are either ageing, already aged, or they are not enough in the labour market.

The irrationality of Canadian experience can be better appreciated by considering a usually small and ignored or peripheral group of migrants in such discussions—artists, be they visual or performing artists, poets, actors, novelists, or dramatists. Here focus is on the creative writer. First, while writing falls under the skills category of "Occupations in Art, Culture Recreation and Sports," it is an open secret that the Canadian immigration point system does not rate creative writing high on its list of professions. However, the culture industry is a viable economic unit like any other industry, requiring expansion and numbers in a country whose small population is a tiny pinhead on its astronomically sized map. Second only to Russia in size, Canada is 1.24 times larger than the USA in total area.

The point is that a creative writer deals in words, which, in any language, do not change conceptually across borders. Canada's store of symbolic capital has been greatly enlarged by the appearance of immigrant writers who are comparable to any other writer of world literature. Examples are M.J. Vasanji, Rohintin Mistry, Austin Clarke, Emma Donoghue, Matha Blum, and Bharati Mukherjee, the last of whom has immigrated further and is now a celebrated American writer and scholar. How shall we define the experience that goes into the literary works produced by the immigrant writer? Certainly, it is not just Canadian experience that shapes their creativity. A writer writes from lived experience, be it Canadian, American, German etc. The immigrant writer is rich in the sense that he or she is a cosmopolitan and his or her experiences are larger than just one small Canadian window. How much has the poet T. S. Elliot, who was born in Missouri, USA, and immigrated to the UK in 1914, improved British literature? Should he have been shut out of opportunities for literary praxis because he was first and foremost an American and thereby forced to become, for example, a banker as he was, or a cobbler? What a loss that would have been for British culture! Coming from America as he did, I am sure no one asked him for British experience before he could write. So, what is this obsession with Canadian experience in the face of globalization?

An ageing global (or Western Hemispheric) economy relies on a random, if regulated and systematic, cross-border movement of people, goods, ideas, and images in order to remain a self-sustaining system. Nowhere should that fact be more urgently acknowledged than in a sparsely populated and ageing Canada, which needs a constant influx of immigrants for self-renewal. Since movement is inherent in our nature considering our hunter-gatherer ancestral beginnings, it falls upon host communities to harness and integrate the productivity, energy, and rich diversity that immigrants bring with them. Canada's ode to local experience marginalizes the immigrant while provincializing Canadian industry.

Literay Essays

Of 'Grammatology' and Writing

Against all first appearances, my concern is not directly with that seminal work titled *Of Grammatology*—Jacques Derrida's 1967 structuralist tome, which is at the intersection of his subsequent deconstructive analyses. Incidentally, that critique has to do with the idea of 'writing' vis-à-vis speech as a subject of philosophical enquiry rather than—of interest here—with writing as compositional praxis. However, an important link can be established between both approaches, namely that the breadth of Derrida's philosophical enquiry can be perceived in, and is therefore necessarily transposable unto, the utilitarian and earthy subject of writing as praxis.

For my purposes, writing is synonymous with meaning or thought and its subsequent explication as text, as 'writing'—the combination of words in sentences to express a simple or complex idea within the rules of traditional grammar. The goal is neither to give writing (as discourse) primacy over speech—as Derrida accuses ethnocentric Western philosophy of having done towards the dismissal of oral cultures—nor is it to make writing a 'direct' translation of 'thought.' It is more a 'transliteration'; hence the necessary idea of writing as 'work' in the process of that transliteration towards arriving at an approximation of what is being thought. That is all quite simple enough, apparently—but not really, if we bring Derrida's basic but complicating logic to bear on that easy equation.

For the deconstructionist, the meaning of a word, which is already an arbitrary convention, is not a static category residing in that particular word but derives from the relative differences between that word and other words; that is, meaning derives from the interplay of differences between word after word after word ad infinitum. It is from this interplay of differences that coherence is bestowed upon the objective world because it helps in delimiting objects or ideas from one another. Such differences occur, of course, at different levels of any one language's grammar: for example, at the primary levels of letters of the alphabets, vowels, morphemes, and syllables, punctuational particles like commas, the period, etc., and the 'unrepresentable'—absent signs such as ellipses. The lexical unit, the word (at a secondary level), is the most visible or immediate moment and realization of such differentiation and meaningfulness. To use words in 'writing,' to form thoughts and be coherent, one has to be aware of the law, or 'grammar,' guiding difference at the primary and secondary levels; hence the idea of a 'grammatology,' a system of grammar literally and metaphorically, a grammar of signs, which understands the rules and negotiates the differences that result in meaning.

'Signs,' here, are not just the words of a language but all other components required to textualise and express thoughts, including graphemes. All of these are brought into a mathematical permutation and combination which results in a textual representation of thought and becomes meaning. The manner of achieving that, once more, is through the recognition of the differences between those items and the rules necessary for negotiating those differences and their proliferation. Again, that system is what I refer to as grammatology. A good understanding and dexterous command and manipulation of the differences within it make such a system functional. It is much like the command a conductor has over and above an orchestra, where the differences in the types of musical instruments and the interplay of their different sounds result in symphonic coherence and harmony. It is clear that such grammatology needs to be learnt from its most rudimentary level to its most complex for a mastery of the skills towards its application in and as writing—a system of arbitrary graphemes or signs whose meaningfulness is always deferred and never present in those signs themselves but is a collocation of all their differences.

As such it is mystifying that—from all evidence—Canadian schools do not teach rudimentary grammar, much less its systematization as 'grammatology.' It is scary that school curricula in English are built around the idea that a native speaker has some almighty linguistic instinct which eschews the need to teach or learn traditional grammar. That is underscored by the North American fallacy of referring to 'pupils' as students!, where the latter term insinuates the absence of real instruction. 'Student' gives the illusion that there is not much learning needed by those so designated, and when they leave high school they are, hyperbolically, high school 'graduates'—conveniently so as to perpetuate the illusion of accomplishment further, even if teachers have not done their job but have limply held these so-called students' limp hands for several fruitless and limp years.

This pedagogic philosophy is one that subscribes to the learning of language 'in use.' Such 'use' is expected to transfer into writing, in lieu of the rules of differentiation, of grammatology. In other words, Canadian schools give speech primacy over writing as 'system.' This is the other extreme of what Derrida accuses Western epistemology of doing—giving writing primacy over speech. In both cases, the result is the misconception that neither writing nor speech—especially as it relates to orality and oral societies—is worthy of study as a system nor has any systematicity. There is the suspicion that Canadian teachers refuse to teach the rules of writing or do not know how to teach it anymore since that tradition of learning was broken several school generations before their own training began or was completed. The devastating import is that a large percentage of the teachers themselves have no knowledge of grammatology or how to impart it to their 'pupils.' It is obvious from the writing skills of the average first-year student at the university level that he or she has been abused with the idea of learning language as 'usage' or 'language in use' as the only preparation for writing. The shortfall is that schools turn out functional illiterates. Concern here is particularly with the English language.

To equate speech with writing as schools do is to short-circuit the process of private reflection and self-immersion in the rules of grammatology that results in good and coherent writing. While the intention is not to suggest the prescriptive in matters of language acquisition, there is still a need to understand the basic workings of it. Suggestions to the contrary are nothing but bad faith and result in grammatical anarchy—the haphazard and unsystematic deployment of words, fragments, slang, and the generally colloquial by the university undergraduate native speaker to whom the grammatology of the mother tongue becomes unfamiliar or vaguely familiar. The result is incoherence, inarticulacy, and frustration for the student, who does not anymore have the high school safety of the five-paragraph essay, and frustration for the classroom and the instructor.

At this point, it is useful to note that grammatology in its original coinage by Ignace Gelb—from whom Derrida borrowed the term—had nothing to do with deconstruction or "differance" but pointed to the physical properties of language as a system of scripts, to their typology, and to the relationship between written and spoken language. Nevertheless, and importantly here, Gelb's original ideas have come to include a study of literacy, the significance of writing for knowledge production from philosophy to religion or the hard sciences, and for social organization. 'Social organization' is important because knowledge production—in how it influences and shapes societal progress—can be seen as a form of it. Based on its social engineering significance, such 'knowledge' and the societies that produce it relative to others are unwittingly hierarchized. It becomes urgent for the 'pupil' and the 'student,' in their gradual socialization, to be good writers towards absorbing, producing or disseminating knowledge, and thereby affecting society progressively. Derrida nods at, and emphasizes, the importance— first inspired by Gelb's work—of the relationship between writing and science—that is, knowledge of all kinds.

That grammatology—the system of the grammar of a language and its application in writing and hence discourse—has overarching ramifications for science, philosophy, and knowledge generally should not be surprising. The reason is not too far-fetched. Language, and its successful manipulation, allows us to give name to things and differentiate between them. As such, the concepts for describing any kind of phenomenon have to be expressed in language—be it even the language of mathematics. The same basic principle of naming and differentiation leading to meaningfulness and conceptual frameworks is at work. Derrida actually places writing as being at the beginning of all science.

The import of this is that a student who does not have a basic mastery of grammatology—in terms of the rules of the combination and permutation of traditional grammar and its complexities—becomes handicapped in knowledge acquisition or dissemination since he or she cannot articulate thoughts with perspicacity. The more complex the thoughts, the more inarticulate a student or speaker of a particular language becomes. This, more or less, turns otherwise impressionable and brilliant young minds towards a wall of fog and perplexity. This is likely to affect their comprehension of other texts, too, since the lack of familiarity with the depth of grammatology means they might not be able to quickly decipher the rules at work in a text, the internal differentiations of which are pointers to comprehension. It affects performance in school and at the university.

It is the case that (especially) 'pupils' at the primary school level are quickly labeled by teachers, who themselves need teaching, as having learning disabilities—slow reading, attention deficit, laziness, lack of zeal, etc. The psychological dimension of a grammatological lack goes so far as to perpetuate a cycle of low self-esteem, ignorance, and poverty—where pupils are forever labeled, become 'institutionalized,' and do not improve themselves further or beyond the artificial limitations imposed by the institution symbolized in the lazy, undiscerning teacher.

The results of lapses in grammatology are crippling for speakers of the language in daily communication situations beyond the classroom, especially when thoughts have to be written down, say, for example, in the simple form of a common letter. The more specialized writing gets, the more ineffective the speaker who has not internalized the rules of grammatology becomes. So, the essay, formal or informal, becomes a headache, and so do other more sophisticated and specialized kinds of writing.

In the absence of grammatology, the import of all this for creative writing could be devastating since the 'extra-linguistic' creativity, which an internalization of grammatology imbues, would be absent. Creative writing would require a familiarity with grammatology as a 'paradigm.' Otherwise, poetry, novels, the essay, and creative non-fiction will become dull versions of what they could be. There is a particular manner in which that could happen.

Apart from the primary level of the alphabet, the vowel, and the phoneme, and the secondary level of words, clauses, sentences, phrases, etc., there is also the less obvious but equally valid syntagmatic and paradigmatic levels of grammatology. Here, the play of differences inheres within syntactical differentiation and coherence and amongst different genres, styles, and themes. At this level, linguistic competence at the primary and secondary levels of grammatology are not enough for creativity. A familiarity with the canon of writing from around the world is useful. It is the same as an awareness and mastery of the primary and secondary levels of grammatology—in terms of a play of differences. This explains the truism that it is only a poor writer who has written more than he or she has read. As such, a 'writer' competent at the primary and secondary level of grammatology might not be so as a 'creative writer' at the syntagmatic and paradigmatic levels, whose chief requirements are an unusual level of 'creative' as opposed to 'linguistic' competence alone.

Syntagma may relate to the internal logic of a literary text, both technical and creative—syntax, theme, plot, and the "moral universe" (to borrow from Chinua Achebe) of the work and the meaning these generate in and amongst themselves in their differences. And the paradigm is marked by the uniqueness of such works and their inter- and intra-genre play of differences within the canon of national or global literature.

On a grammatological level of the syntagma and within the paradigm of poetry for example, one finds a lot of contemporary Canadian, and indeed North American, writing rather aping prose. To disarm the critic, such poetry is quickly presented as 'prose poetry.' It is not to say there could not be some innovative and sincere form of that kind. But with the examples out there such (oxy) morons as 'prose poetry' leave the structure of the syntagmatic and try to jump onto the paradigmatic axis; that is, their syntax is that of prose, even though the intended paradigm is poetry. But at the same time, they do not fit into the paradigm of fiction. Such a grammatological weakness can be found in various forms in other genres of creative writing. Reading widely and selectively can be a useful way to avoid such traps of literary writing.

Reading widely—which, at the syntagmatic and paradigmatic levels, stands in for a more basic morphological kind of grammatology as in the school essay—does not merely refer to the reading of literature in whatever genre only. It also points to the reading of cultures generally, of which literature is only an aspect. It is in this sense that Canadian writing sometimes becomes provincial (pun intended), with its tendency for the hyper-narcissistic, and ultra-micro-nisation—'New Brunswick writing,' 'Albertan writing,' and other such stringent compartmentalizing. Such writing completely ignores the marrying of the local and the national, or the national and the global. Its themes, plots, and narrative strategies completely eschew the grammatological impetus of the global. This is not to say that writing 'deliberately' set to emphasize the local is not valid, but that making it the goal and sole purpose of regional or national literature is a bit extreme.

Canadian literature need not be 'a literature of the provinces'; it should dialogue more with each other across the Rockies and the Prairies; interact with other writing from across North America and the globe. Fortunately, Canada, irrespective of its near total geographical isolation except for the USA as neighbour, still has a rich cultural advantage in a population that is at once local and global. Canadians come from all corners of the earth and bring their imagination with them. Nevertheless, for Canadian literature to exploit the possibilities in differences towards a rich literary and cultural diversity, it has to shed some of its provinciality, shun a tendency towards elitism, and be more open to an influx of new, replenishing blood. The literary world is right here in Canada, and the country's literary self-constitution can only be strengthened by immigrant difference. To enable that, the teaching of grammatology has to be taken up again as a serious project by schools. This is necessary for practical linguistic reasons on the one hand and, on the other, for life-changing lessons in a philosophy of differences, which is already a cherished Canadian value and the very essence of Canadian socio-political life.

An emphasis on that philosophy can only prepare new generations of Canadian writers and secure the future of Canadian literature in a global cultural arena and knowledge circuit.

Bakhtin the Poet

In his seminal essay, "Epic and the Novel," on the concept of 'heteroglossia,' Mikhail Bakhtin insists that the novel is the only literary form still evolving; that it carries the future development or elaboration of all literature within its kernel through its open-endedness and its peculiar ability to incorporate other closed-ended genres—like the epic or even tragedy—within it. The novel's vaunted permeability, its inclusiveness, and its celebration of the carnivalesque is the bedrock of his thesis on heteroglossia. In comparison, other genres are moribund and dead as far as extending their literary parameters go, and even if they did strive for self-expansion, they could only do so within their hermetically sealed circle or, at best, end up breaking out of their orbits to stretch out and mimic the novel's linear projection; they would become 'novelised.' The novel is polyglot, many voiced, and democratising in its impact on the spirit of the letter and, in consequence, on society.

The Epic, in its ancient and oral roots in preliterate societies, has been originally associated with poetry of course; a poetry usually sung to music and sometimes later written down when particular societies became literate. Usually, the older the epic, the more certain it is to be steeped in orature; and the closer it is to contemporary times, the more it becomes the literary epic. Every society started out as preliterate and oral, such that most cultures have these epics. As in the 'world folk-epic'—they can sometimes be the informing worldview or Weltanschauung of social contracts, in which case they are similar to what Bakhtin rightly refers to as the 'national' epic. There is more to this, but in a moment.

Bakhtin concentrated on the emergence of the epic in the Western tradition, as might be expected considering that he grew up in the
West; nevertheless, one would have expected the researcher in him to
either include variations to his European model or delimit its universalist posturing. This is one of the occlusions (perhaps inadvertent) of his
analysis, which heavily privileges the Western tradition. Examples of
the epic in this tradition are *Beowulf, The Iliad, The Odyssey,* and *Paradise Lost.* In the East, we have the *Mahabarata, Ramayan,* and *Shan-
ama,* and in ancient Africa *The Epic of Gilgamesh* and others like *The
Epics of Sundjata, The Lianja Epic* and the *Silmaka Epic.* The most
recent contemporary epic poetry—a literary rather than oral epic—is
from the Caribbean: Derek Walcott's *Omeros,* published in 1990 and
intertextual to the oral Greek epic, which was written down later as
The Odyssey. This listing is far from exhaustive. Important is the fact
that, in every single corner of the earth where human beings have lived,
East, West, North, or South, there has been one or several such epics
produced, the oldest known epic being the Sumerian epic mentioned
above, *Gilgamesh,* written by Shin-eqi-unninni and dated at 2000 BC,
older than probably all other known epics and coming from pre-his-
torical African roots. The question here is: why does Bakhtin occlude
the account of the epic from all over the face of the earth and adopt the
Western epic as a model for discussion, while dismissing the epic generally as a literary form as being close-ended? Before this is addressed,
let us go back to the idea of the 'national epic.'

Bakhtin considers the epic a romantic look over the shoulders of
the nation, a kind of narcissistic pining for a lost world or for mythol-
ogising the nation's self. In its project, then, the national epic naturally uses what Bakhtin refers to as a "national language." This does
not point to any referent in the real world but is an allegory for the
modes of the epic's self-mythologising exfoliation; for the tongue of
the epic, which tongue does not have any one locale in any particular

mouth? The allegory is a major trope in the epic form, and as such Bakhtin behaves like a poet while in the same breath dismissing the epic form, and thus poetry itself, as having "congealed" beyond any further development. It does not allow inclusiveness like the novel; it alienates other genres and by extension it is not subversive of, nor does it democratise, those hierarchies in society, of which it is—as the 'high art' of petit bourgeoisie authority—symbolic. As a matter of fact, the chief rhetorical strategies in "Epic and the Novel" are the symbol, allegory, metaphor, and metonymy —usually tropes that are very central to, and are the very breath of, poetry. Such signifiers as national language (allegory), a "valorised hierarchy of genres" (metonymy standing in for the hierarchies within society itself), and so on, have no specific referent in the real world. They are abstract concepts that can only be unpacked through a recourse to the liberating language of poetry!; a very dialogic form that allows the novel to come into being in the first place. I would say that poetry is the only possible engine for prose of any kind, whether the artistic prose to which Bakhtin referred—that is the novel—or to creative non-fiction, the biography, the essay—ordinary or literary—or even the common letter. Since some concepts can be abstract, the mind needs the 'image' in order to elucidate a point or idea or thought. The 'image' is the unit of poetry, and good poetry excites all kinds of images and appeals to the senses in a near palpable manner. All rhetorical tropes exist towards such elucidation of thought. This is why philosophers across the ages fall into the same kind of platonic trap such as the one Bakhtin springs on himself. Plato would have the Poet arrested and crucified for dealing in dreams and images, but Plato, in explaining his abstract ideas, needed images to make them clear; he was guilty of behaving like a poet, of using language like a poet. His cave allegory is an example of such contradictions as a critic like Paul Hamilton has noted in *New Historicism*.

To further elaborate on Bakhtin's conflation of poetry with rigidity in form and its presumed lack of dialogue with other forms, one·could take a closer look at his thesis in a related essay, "Rabelais and His World." There he brings his theory of heteroglossia to bear on Rabelais' novel, *Pantagruel*. He shows how the author's deployment of the language of parody in a setting of medieval carnival travesties the usual hierarchical order of civic life. *Pantagruel* levels all discourses in the derisive laughter of the marketplace feast, where social rank is erased by mockery. The laughter that he proposes as the energy of the levelling processes within social hierarchies and official truths in the novel should have been preceded by a cry—he should have elaborated his own metaphor or image—that is, extended it with 'the spontaneous cry of being alive,' and 'the sudden realisation of consciousness', which are what poetry is! It is the cry of a child being born into the world, exulting in its existence on the one hand, and allowing the child to progress to speech as it grows on the other. The child is poetry—when it grows to a boy or girl it becomes the novel. They are one and the same, and their destinies are infinitely interwoven. That cry is the cry of poetry while the novel merely laughs. Without the cry there cannot be laughter. It is that cry of the soul—as in the poignancy of the language of poetry—which peters out to levels off into a laughter of conciliation, inclusion and of mutual self-deprecation around the scene of the travesties during the medieval feast. This then challenges social order, power, or prestige, and lets in the dialogism extolled by Bakhtin.

Again, one notes Bakhtin's deployment of symbols, metaphor, and images in his diction in "Rabelais and His World"—'laughter' (which image I have made into a sustained metaphor above); masks (representing the assumption and reversals of roles during the carnival); the scatological images of the lower parts of the body (i.e., a metonymy for the commoners) challenging the upper part of the body (i.e., metonymy for medieval European aristocracy) on the one hand, and also insisting on its importance in the general regeneration of the whole body, on the other. The lower parts must be in dialogue with the upper for the whole organism to regenerate. Thus, we can see how through this array of rhetorical strategies, Bakhtin becomes a poet unwittingly.

To go back to the question which I raised in the first paragraph: why has Bakhtin occluded examples of carnival in other societies of the world, privileged the European brand, and then gone ahead to insinuate it as a meta-narrative for all cultures? Apart from the very observant comment by Terry Eagleton that the European ruling class gives its blessings to the feast, allowing the medieval carnival to happen exactly in order to diffuse the plebeian source of threat to its hegemony, it is possible to conjecture that Bakhtin was in the grip of that blinding enlightenment endorsement of the repression of other parts of the world by the Europe of his own day—in short, that he was in the grip of an enlightenment ideology. Carnival as a form of travesty of all manner of social hierarchies exists in other cultures, the mockery of normative order being just one of them. Such mockery of class and privilege is not merely only from the bottom up but can take place on the same social level—say as between women in the age-old Western Nigerian 'Oke'Ibadan' festival where, for example, women wear straps of huge penises to parody their husband's and general male phallic power and thereby travesty it, emphasising a penis-upending upended (pun intended) world of social relations and rollicking in the power inversions of the moment in the following limericks:

> Odo do do mi
> Ko ma ma je un sun o

Oba mi wa wo irun obo mi
Meta lo ku o!

meaning:

He screwed me and screwed me
And would not let me sleep
O Lordy, look at my pubic hairs
There are only
three strands left from the chaffing!

And this is just one scene of possible locales of humour, parody, travesty, inversion, subversion, and the dialogue ensuing from that inversion; oppressed and oppressor are participant in this Yoruba carnival, accompanied by gay laughter. It is the general relaxed environment of the prose—not the cry of the gruelling gender inequality—of the quotidian. It is noteworthy, too, that the daily dose of shame about sexuality and taboos are suspended/upended. The woman is free to talk like 'a whore' if she is so inclined and right in her husband's face too, or even pursue the male with a gargantuan phallus strapped around the waist in a mimicry of female rape. This ritual is age-old and must have existed at the time Bakhtin wrote his essay. And such carnivals existed in other parts of the world, surely. Definitely, it existed in the Caribbean, where inversion was necessary for the slave's very self-preservation. Such carnivals were not only ritualistic in the Caribbean and Africa; they were also linguistic. The linguistic forms of it led to the inversion of the English language into—respectively— Patios, Creole, and Pidgin English (in Nigeria and most of west Africa).

The medieval European was definitely not as oppressed as the slave on a sugar plantation in the West Indies; so why does Bakhtin conveniently occlude such other scenes of oppression? Again, the only answer can be that he was part and parcel of a universalist enlightenment discourse, which assumed Europe to be the centre of the universe, the place on the universal power grid from which electric bolts of knowledge travel outwards into the dark spaces of the world. Bakhtin was a man of his time. And it is particularly insulting for critics to suggest using a Bakhtinian model or concept of carnival in explaining cultural phenomenon in the contemporary Caribbean and Latin America as well as in Asia and Africa (which are far older cultures). The African mask, for example, beyond the ritual of mimicry and play, has deeply esoteric import for the one wearing a mask; or put differently, there are playful masks—masks of role inversions—and other masks that have a mathe-magical significance for the wearer, who is instantly connected to an esoteric, extra-worldly dimension. To wear a mask in a West African Carnival is to inhabit a different psychic space, to cross the thresholds of this world and commune with the ancestors. It is the very steep of poetry; it is going back to the cry. To occlude these other forms of carnival is not dialogic!; it is anti-heteroglossia, it is monologic.

Bakhtin's heteroglossia has a shredded tongue, one that forgets its origins, the deep chassis of the mouth where it is still deeply buried—inside poetry. A novel cannot exist without poetry: its proposed dialogism is only allowed by the accents it learnt from poetry. Bakhtin himself is in the death grip of ideology in the Althusserian sense in his discourse of dialogism; in an Althusserian sense because Bakhtin probably never knew he was serving the hierarchies he sought to dismantle with his theory.

Wit and Witticisms

English poetics of the Augustan period, that is, from the 17th through the 18th century, was ambivalent about the deployment of wit—'false wit'—in its poetry particularly and in prose generally. In Roger D. Lund's "The Ghosts of Epigram, False Wit, and the Augustan Mode," he refers to George Williamson (1961), who quotes Robert South thus: "[b]revity and succinctness of speech is that, which in philosophy or speculation, we call *maxim*, and first principle; in the counsels and resolves of practical wisdom, and the deep mysteries of religion, *oracle*; and lastly, in matters of wit, and the finenesses of imagination, *epigram*."

Generally, an epigram is a short witty saying; but in the Augustan sense, it could be an epigrammatic couplet standing as a stanza or a longer short poem in couplets as a legitimate form within a hierarchy including the epic, the dramatic, the lyric, the elegiac, the epigrammatic, and the bucolic. Lund notes that the epigram was the most problematic in rhetorical legitimacy for the critics of the day, like John Dryden, Joseph Addison, or even Alexander Pope, who nevertheless wrote several epigrams himself and who, according to J. Paul Hunter, "brought the couplet—already the dominant form of English poetry for more than a century—[and one of the chief characteristics of the epigram] to its most finished state of formal perfection and at the same time popularized its accessible conversational ease." Before we proceed, here is an example from Pope's "Essay on Criticism:

A little Learning is a dang'rous Thing;
Drink deep, or taste not the Pierian Spring:

There shallow Draughts intoxicate the Brain,
And drinking largely sobers us again.

Although those lines are excerpted from a much longer poem and were not composed in the usual short-form epigrams come in—especially in the epigrammatic epitaph—it can nevertheless stand alone as an epigram. It is complete as an epigram, with a rhyming couplet (or the heroic couplet), equivocation in the first line, the pun in 'draughts' juxtaposed with 'drinking', and closure and surprise in the last line where the drunken becomes magically sober from more drinking. The ring of the first line sounds like a maxim or a truth, although it is built on the fiction, sloganeering, and myth of the Pierian spring; its truth is closer to fiction than to that of logic, philosophy, or science. Now let us take another example from the same 'Wit'—for these poets with such quicky turns of sharp utterances were also referred to as wits:

See how the World its Veterans rewards!
A Youth of frolicks, an old Age of Cards,
Fair to no purpose, artful to no end,
Young without Lovers, old without a Friend,
A Fop their Passion, but their Prize a Sot,
Alive, ridiculous, and dead, forgot!

The above is quoted by Lund, who notes the emphasis on antithesis—common in Pope, for example in the long poem, "Essay on Man," and in the Augustan epigram generally—which we can equate with the equivocation in the first example due to the similarity in rhetorical move.

Such was the hold of the epigram on the 18th century that, despite its "equat[ion] with the exploitation of puns and conceits that everyone conceded to be forms of false wit," it was neverthe-less difficult to exorcise the poetic imagination of the day of what, in the first place, made it 'witty.' One reason for the paradox can be deduced from Hunter's assertion that there was a grey area between writing and talking in the 18th century and that active conversa-tion was an art that was cultivated and diligently pursued in coffee-houses—especially in the city. As such, the close approximation of the Augustan epigram to everyday speech—embellished with antithesis, with couplets and equivocations, with 'the point' or clo-sure and surprise and humour—had popular appeal; besides, these epigrams were the main content of "miscellanies", which were 'textbooks' on cultivated speech and 'universal truths' and a part of the education of young men of class. This popularity made it easy to simply anchor formal metric features onto popular speech, insin-uating a sophistication of wit—for all it is worth—with the results passing for elevated literary speech, while managing to maintain the distinction between prose proper and poetry.

There was also the allure that the epigram was easy to remem-ber, especially where knowledge of aphoristic universals was con-cerned. Again, it should be noted that such 'truths' were neverthe-less based on false logic. If we juxtapose the scientific deduction, 'twelve inches make one foot' with Pope's "A little learning is a dangerous thing," the first term would be much more accurate math-ematically (and could be proven logically) than the second. Perhaps it is one reason why Plato wanted to kick the poet out of his repub-lic, although poetry does, of course, have as its function in the culti-vation of the mind and humanizing of the man or woman.

Augustan 'false' wit, with its "anagrams, acrostics, jests, rid-dles, rebuses, conundrums, epigrams, and cheap witticisms," is not the kind of wit one intends to dwell upon in this essay. But before we depart this course of investigation, we ought to have one more

example from a modernist, namely T.S. Eliot; a paraphrase will do:
"Your husband is coming to dinner tonight/may it be the last that he
shall eat!" This is from one of Eliot's minor poems, and he was wise
in not pursuing such epigrammatic fancies in his major poems or in
the larger body of his oeuvre. Finally, the simplest way for the contemporary mind to grasp the worst of Augustan wit is to compare it
to what we would call the limerick today. In short, the epigram was
too unserious a form to be totally integrated into the major forms,
except the burlesque, the ribald, or the comic.

To grasp the kind of wit in contemplation, we should begin with
the 'true wit' of the Greeks as distinct from that Latinate impostor
introduced by Martial Ausonius and dealing in antithesis, equivocation, closure or 'point,' and surprise, which are the direct progenitor
of Augustan false wit. Greek wit was, mostly, a set of fine thoughts;
it neither dealt in mirth nor surprise but could give aesthetic pleasure to fragile sensibilities. What was required of the Greek epigram
was a simple brevity and unity of thought. Such brevity and unity
of thought, which can be achieved with a lean syntax, imagistic and
precise diction, and poignancy, is the kind of wit under consideration.

Those qualities can then be instrumental toward the function of
organic unity within a poem. The contemporary poet should then
always question himself or herself about the purpose of a word or
an expression within the poem. A superfluity of wording or expression should be shunned since it could lead to prosaicness at best,
mixed metaphors at worst, or, catastrophically, a complete breakdown of intended verbal and thematic effects. Here, there is a need
to comment on the over-elaborately brief. There is such a thing
as false economy in traditional grammar just as in the syntax of
poetry. While writing about the new-fangled 'plunderverse,' Gregory Betts in "Plunderverse: A Cartographic Manifesto" gave the
example of a two-word poem and proceeds to confidently refract

its import through a specific cultural prism. The poem in question is bpNichol's "Catching Frogs": "jar din." That is the whole poem; yes, "Jar din"! Gregory Betts then justifies with:

> His brilliant "Catching Frogs," for instance, unravels
> an entire narrative with just two words: "jar din."
> From the bilingual play of the two words, the activ-
> ity (catching frogs) gains a locus (the garden) and a
> conclusion (the frog is now in the jar). Best of all, the
> title plays on the pun of frogs as Frenchmen, and the
> game of finding French words in English.

Ellipsis or omission is a normal trope in poetry—and a useful one too, which helps in streamlining syntax and scintillating the cerebrum of the reader; nevertheless, there is usually some hint or a clue for the reader, some sort of scaffolding, narrow as it might be, for a reader to walk upon towards comprehension. None is apparent here, except perhaps in the title. Even then there are cultural and linguistic barriers set up here for a speaker who knows only English. The intended pun on 'frogs as Frenchmen"—obvious as it might seem to North American readers—and "the game of finding French words in English," are too culturally specific to be transparent to speakers of English elsewhere. It would have served the poet's purpose better to construct the line such that the brevity is retained, but not at the expense of the mono-lingual reader. There is also the possibility of miscomprehension even for the North American reader of English. "Jar din" could be read merely as an anagram of 'garden' without the reader making any conclusive semantic deductions— except, perhaps, with the weak prop of the titling, which might suggest to him or her that someone is catching physical frogs in the garden and that there is a 'din' (noise) in the 'jar' where the frogs are dropped. The punning insinuated in the bilingualism would be lost due to a cultural opacity. It is indeed a brilliant ploy but one that leaves too much room for ambiguity, unless the poet intended to append footnotes! This is brevity at its most unnecessarily extreme. But of course, Betts is discussing avant-garde experimental or language poetry, which probes the limits of a language that we are "forced into."

That language is arbitrary and difficult to master does not mean that there are no agreed units, rules, and modes of signification. Once we learn the signs in a particular language, such a language's arbitrariness is then delimited by rules of communication. A structuralist fallacy of eternal arbitrariness can then be unmasked. We do use words to mean something, irrespective of whether words are arbitrary or not; words, that is, in syntactical relationships within a sentence or a line of verse. Contractions, in the form of syntactical brevity or ellipses, should expand the field of signification through its omissions and not raise cultural semantic blocks, semantic ambiguity, or doubts. Otherwise, such constructions would fall under what one might call 'witticisms,' though perhaps not quite the 'false wit' of the Augustan epigram since the tropes involved and effects intended or achieved may be different.

For our purposes, witticisms are forms, which (through the instrument of figures and syntactical constructions other than that of Augustan poetics; or a mixture of the latter's features and different or similar contemporary tropes) begin to bend towards the false wit of Augustan poetics. In this model, the above example of an over-contraction of a poem would be a witticism; so too would be the lipogram because it relies on a preponderance of phonic punning and, like the Augustan epigram and its conceits, resembles what Sir William Temple, according to Lund, in complaining about the influence of Martial on the Augustan period, describes as:

an Ingredient that gave Taste to Compositions which
had little of themselves; 'twas a Sauce that gave Point
to Meat that was Flat, and some Life to Colours that
were Fading. . . . However it were, this Vein first over-
flowed our modern [read contemporary] Poetry, and
with so little Distinction or Judgment that we would
have Conceit as well as Rhyme in every Two Lines,
and run through all our long Scribbles as well as the
short, and the whole Body of the Poem, whatever it is.

Temple's observation would apply to most areas of the contemporary avant-garde. For example, Augustan Poetry—as insinuated
by Hunter—emphasized "special representations on the page like
symmetrical rectangles ... or other repeated shapes." He contends
that modern poetry, meaning poetry as it is today, shuns the overt
rhyme and does not call attention to its shape and patterns of repeti-
tion. We must assume that Hunter has not read much of the contemporary avant-garde! Perhaps, he has not read much concrete poetry.

The avant-garde overreaches itself in the phenomenon of the
plunderverse, which purports to save the 'waste' of language by
creating poems from other already finished text by other poets. It is
not a parody, no; nor is plunderverse satisfied with intertextuality or
the literary allusion, but it must tear down other texts completely to
make its perverse points; it simply plunders! These language games
do not represent true innovation or experiments, nor do they show
much originality. There are also issues of ethics and copyright to be
considered. This kind of literary narcissism is not much different
from what the Augustan period practised to an extreme and which
made several critics of the day cry out, 'foul'!

Experiments in language are necessary and useful but not in the
form of witticisms, which introduce a cultural decadence similar to

what 'the age of Martial' initiated into 18th century thought. One way in which witticisms in poetry introduce cultural decadence is that they impact the language in which they are written in a negative way; more on that shortly. According to Betts, and as it is common knowledge, Shakespeare influenced the English language by introducing new words into it through his poetic utterances—one thousand and seven hundred new words exactly, two of which are 'excellence' and 'majestic.' In the same way, contemporary poets, depending on their originality—and 'wit' in the proper sense or witticisms, as the case might be—may influence any language by introducing not only new words but turns of expressions, which then flow into the general current of a living language. Since language is the medium for expressing cultural thought, subjective reality can be influenced by writers in general and poets particularly. Politics is one area of culture where the accretions from writers and poets, especially poets, may be used or abused by power to shape subjective reality for ill or even for good—but most times for ill.

We can now begin to closely look at the specific ways in which the contemporary avant-garde (with its perverse witticisms), or the poetaster and the lazy poet may, like Martial in previous centuries, initiate cultural decay and shape and mis-shape subjectivities. The linguistic gestures of the poet in any language, once they flow into the mainstream, are likely to find unconscious replication in the users of that language. This is an age of war, of religious belligerence and bigotism; these two areas of cultural life are then very sensitive to such influences from poets, or writers generally. The war in Iraq was initiated through the agency of language first—that is, the language of propaganda or perverse rhetoric. When a powerful leader of the world uses the expression, "the axis of evil"—whether borrowed from a speechwriter or not—he is following one of the rhetorical strategies (metonymy in this case) of the poet.

The expression is witty in a negative 18th century epigrammatic fashion. It takes hold of the naïve subject with the force of the slogan, though based on untruth; it is short, witty, and therefore memorable. The metonymy, 'axis of evil,' neatly cuts the world into two different opposed parts with the certitude of a samurai sword. There are several binaries at work there, good and evil being just one of them. The listener can then go on, depending on their political sway, and imaginatively multiply such binaries: Muslim=bad and Christian =good, and so on. Binaries are dangerous because they leave the mind in a stupor and close all doors to mediating discourses. In this way, the war was first fought (and won for propaganda) on the level of language before its physical manifestation. And when one bellicose leader taunts another and promises him 'the mother of all battles,' again the rhetorical gesture consolidated by countless poets in ages past is put into a negative use.

Of course, it is easy to argue that the metonymy and the prepositional construction exemplified are a standard in any language, are parts of our linguistic unconscious already, and are available to anyone who would abuse it. Very true, and this is precisely why the poet should not further deploy expressions—heavy on false wit or witticisms, illogic, and untruth—which may become mainstream in the future of any language; rather, have truth and reason at the writing elbow, such that there will be no rhetorical precedence for misappropriation; or that if false wit should occur in utterance, the very structure and character of a language would make it obvious at once.

Contemporary avant-garde's witticisms—and here one should include not only the verbal but also 'representational witticisms' such as drawings, irrational textual form, or mixed media—as they are deployed lead to cultural decay by impoverishing what could otherwise be examples of great poetry for tradition and by pushing language inexorably into a dead-end, even if the avant-garde thinks it is doing the exact opposite. Due to false wit, there is plenty room for a political misappropriation of rhetoric. Let us take the example of the Plunderverse rhetorical manifesto according to Betts:

> Plunderverse limits its own expression to the source text, but attempts a genuine, divergent expression through the selection, deletion or contortion of it. Plunderverse makes poetry through other people's words. The constraint is not random, but merely an accelerated variation of the basic fact of language: we already speak in each other's words. Plunderverse exaggerates the constraints through which we realize and discover our own voice, re-enacting the struggle against influences and cultural histories. It does not try to obscure, bury or overcome influence, but, in fact, celebrates the process by which influences vary into and inform our own voices. It foregrounds the process of language acquisition, reveals the debt of influence and exploits the waste of language.

Underlying the above manifesto is another kind of witticism, non-verbal but equally dangerous, namely that of legitimising theft and destruction, this time literary destruction and theft as distinct from borrowing, allusion, or intertextuality—and by extension, any kind of theft and destruction. There is a moral hole at the centre of this 'plundering' that is appalling. It seeks to deface an already finished work under the fallacy that we speak in each other's words, anyway. Betts occludes the fact that even if we utter each other's words, they come out with differing tonal ranges and combinations that do not make any two sentence the exact same thing. It is indeed wastage if someone were to take my poetry and, through cancellation and selection, pretend to have 'written' a new 'original' poem. Plunderverse exemplifies the laziness that powers the avant-garde, as it is now constituted, by promoting or seeking to atrophy personal imagination and true creative impulse. It celebrates war and despoliation—literally, war on words and, metaphorically, war as a 'phenomenon' in itself—and as a means of balance in wasteful and over-producing economies. Listen to him:

> As Bataille wrote, economies that depend upon wastefulness must obscure the waste or risk the insurgence of destabilization. The Vikings, in their indelicate raids, pillaged the excesses of communities without destroying the waste-producing structures (allowing them to return and plunder again in the future).

Should one walk into a gallery and begin to take bits and pieces of a painting to create a collage of another painting. The new work would amount to a destruction and theft of the old. Surely one would be flogged out of the gallery as Jesus Christ flogged religious whores out of the synagogues of his youth.

True wit should deploy syntactical brevity, measured cadence, memorable expression, and even the pun, but all within an ambience of truthful utterance developed through demonstrable logic and not empty binarisms, antithesis, or the maxim; it should not provide wayward moral injunctions in its subtext.

The Professional Poet?

Is it possible, strange as it may sound in the fiercely capitalist economy of the quotidian, that there exists such a creature as a professional poet today—perhaps in certain parts of the world? Obvious as it might appear, it is nevertheless necessary to emphasize that by 'professional poet' my reference is to those who do nothing else for a living but write poetry and live by its proceeds—which will surely be close to nothing! If this economic wonder does exist, is the professional poet not destined for the doghouse—or shall we call it pigsty, reminiscent of the prodigal son in the Bible who must steal from the pigs and eat their food? Apart from the basic necessities of subsisting in a competitive economy, it is not impossible that some poets, weaned on 'the image' as they are, can relish the sensuous to an extreme, be keen as sword-blades, and love to live life to the scabbard-hilt; as such, there has to be an absent but prospectively magnanimous father-surrogate for whom he or she would be a literary 'foundling.' Literary patronage is as old as writing itself. We can go as far back as ancient Rome to find examples.

Ancient Rome's patronage system was diverse and not only involved the literary arts but also embraced the whole society in a pyramid of dependency, at the top of which was the king (during the imperial period). There were literary, social, and communal gradations on this pyramid; emphasis is on the cultural—that is, the literary. A client-patron (cliens-patronus) relationship was mediated by the writer or poet's financial straits and the desire for immortality by the patron—powerful, aristocratic, or famous, who was nevertheless scared of losing all that to the oblivion of death. Poets after all could immortalize him in verse or prose, dedicate works to him, or even augment his public positions while he lived and breathed. Yes, there were politics involved, too. The poet could consolidate a patron's political or social position by augmenting in verse the latter's profile in the former's work. It was a mutually beneficial position for patron and poet alike. In ancient Rome, the poet did not receive any royalties and had to pay for and even distribute his own works by himself, so having a rich and powerful patron was useful in promoting the writer and imbuing the patron with prestige (while alive) and immortality (while dead).

Publius Vergilius Maro, that is, Virgil, Horace or Quintus Horatius Flaccus, and Propertius, also known as Sextus Propertius, all enjoyed the promotion and support of Gaius Maecenas, famous patron of the arts in the Roman world and a close associate of Emperor Augustus. Virgil's Aeneid propagated a god-like Augustus, presenting him as an almost divine ruler; Horace's odes sing the defeat of Cleopatra and Marcus Antonius in Actium at the hands of Augustus. In a world built by slaves, a patron could sometimes raise the social position of slave or serf who happens also to be a writer. An example was Terence Lucanus, who was a senator and patronized Publius Terence Afer, slave-playwright of African origin. But our focus is on the poet particularly. And this brings us to Shakespeare—known for his plays mostly, but he was also a remarkable poet.

Shakespeare had not just one but a whole group of patrons, made up of figures drawn from the aristocracy of the day. The Walsingham-Sidney-Pembroke-Excess literary circle promoted not only Shakespeare, though, but a group of poets and writers. The group was referred to either as the Excess or the Wilton Circle, depending on which of those two places it met. Of course, some of Shakespeare's works were dedicated to those members of the aris-tocracy who supported him—for example, the long poems "Venus and Adonis" and the "Rape of Lucrece" are dedicated to the Earl of Southampton, Henry Wriothesley. Through the agency of the poet, the politician is indeed immortal!

Unlike in ancient Rome, where the poet was an unofficial megaphone of the State, medieval England, since the time of James I, has installed a Poet Laureate who was sworn informally to propagating the monarch's political ambitions and formally to composing poems for official and personal royal functions like births, deaths, and so on. The position of Poet Laureate grew from an ancient custom where the King had minstrels and versifiers attached to his household.

For centuries, since Charles II, a laureate was installed for life. Randomly, one can point to Geoffrey Chaucer, Edmund Spencer, Ben Johnson, and John Dryden as notable Poet Laureates of the medieval, Tudor, Stuart, and early modern periods respectively. It is only since the early modern period that there exists a formal office of Poet Laureate in England; otherwise, poets were simply adopted or employed by the King as part of his retinue.

The existence of court poets is not confined to the West alone. In fact, it probably has its roots in oral cultures and is as old as society in its rudimentary stages. Such that in oral African cultures, the court poet was an integral part of royal court life; the only difference here to the medieval, early modern, and modern European cultures being that the African court poet was a performer in the sense that he verbalized rather than wrote down—even with the accompaniment of a simple musical instrument or a lone horn—the praises of the King as handed down from generations of other court poets or traditional lore. Modern African traditional performance poets, like Lanre Adepoju, now employ a complex of guitars, traditional drums, and other modern instruments in rendering traditional poetry. The main point here is that like the old English poets, ancient and

modern traditional African poets employ poetry in praise of the
monarch and are a normal part of official and unofficial court-life.

Were these then professional poets? The answer to that is complex and debatable. Clearly the fortunes of the old poets of the Western written tradition were not as strongly dependent on the English
kings as much and as completely as that of traditional African poets
were tied to the purse strings of African Monarchs. We do know
that some English poets—for example, William Morris, William
Mason, Thomas Gray, Sir Walter Scott, and, recently in 1984, Philip
Larkin—did reject the poet laureateship of England. But is such a
life possible today for a poet; such a life of waiting for the crumbs,
grain, and dribble from lordly tables? For one, the poet's relationship to the audience is much more distant today than in the days of
active sponsoring monarchies and direct private patronage.

In late 19th century Europe, the relationship of the poet to
the public became mediated through the phenomenon of the literary market due to the rise of the middle class. Direct personal
patronage dwindled. Poets such as Wordsworth began to complain about public dictates on the themes of their work. It was
the period when the term "intellectual" first entered the dictionary
and such new-fangled diction as "genius" sprang up. The image
of a 'romantic artist,' who was self-willed and self-directed and
above the vagaries of the private 'control' of the court, money-ed
gentry, or a general soliciting public, was created in the public
domain. Contemporary literary culture has inherited this apparent independence in the figure of the poet; it is 'apparent' only
because other patronage systems—like prize-awarding institutions, writers' organisations, book clubs, and enduring national
laureateships in the West—have been put in place by civil society. To what extent do such institutions control what the poet produces? First, we should look at the possibility of self-subversion

inherent in the ancient Roman patronage system and then relate it to the same syndrome today.

Trevor Fear (1993), quoting Carson, mentions "the dilemma of the artist in a money economy" (75). He makes specific reference to Ovid's deployment of the trope of pimping and prostitution regarding the poet and the poem respectively. According to Fear, Leslie Kurke suggests that Pindar tried to negotiate a safe passage between money and corruption through investing his own promotion by the aristocracy with a noble, genteel, and sensible use of money. Fear notes that Horace was also anxious and tried in his poems Epistles 1.17 and 1.18 to represent the poet as *matrona fidelis* and not *levis*. Self-serving rhetoric this must have been, especially if the poet abdicated his duty to the society as social critic and the rallying point for cultural progress. Pindar projected the idea that the Roman nobility was merely a kind friend! Well, we know about the brutality of the Roman domination of those spaces it conquered. Were the poets guilty or not of complicity? The model should be that of the African traditional court bard or griot, who not only sings the King's praises but also daubs him in slime and spittle—although through the subterfuge of intricate linguistic decoys—when it is necessary. Akintunde Akinyemi, in a study of the satirical impregnation of Yoruba court poetry, shows how the paid piper still piped to his patron's disadvantage with the use of sophisticated literary tropes. When it was necessary, the Oba or King was the subject of ridicule or criticism by his court bard. Can this be said for the professional poet of today? If poets' livelihoods depend on prizes, Nobel or Ignoble, awards, laureateships, grants, and institutional-cum academic appointments based on their oeuvre alone, then yes, they are professional poets; they subvert self and their art—unless they are still capable of dispensing their usual critical duties. Otherwise, the professional poets are forced to sing the tunes expected of them and play up to a gallery of politicians, literary administrators, the beguiled or ignorant public, and so on.

When poets insist on discharging their duties to the society by being overtly critical, they fall out of favour or power. Power should not be their preserve anyway because power corrupts and so does money; and these two are infinitely entwined in the game of patronage. Humility, not the monarch's chambers, should be the poet's first court. A good example of a poet falling out of favour is the erstwhile Poet Laureate of New Jersey, Amiri Baraka, who was brave enough, in a world running wild with lap-dog poets, to criticize. Here is the poem in contention:

Somebody Blew up America

They say it's some terrorist,
some barbaric
A Rab,
in Afghanistan
It wasn't our American terrorists
It wasn't the Klan or the Skin heads
Or the them that blows up nigger
Churches, or reincarnates us on Death Row
It wasn't Trent Lott
Or David Duke or Giuliani
Or Schundler,
Helms retiring...
Who killed the most niggers
Who killed the most Jews
Who killed the most Italians
Who killed the most Irish
Who killed the most Africans

Who killed the most Japanese
Who killed the most Latinos...
Who knew the World Trade Center was gonna get
bombed
Who told 4000 Israeli workers at the Twin Towers
To stay home that day
Why did Sharon stay away..?
Like an Owl exploding
In your life in your brain in your self
Like an Owl who know the devil
All night, all day if you listen,
Like an Owl
Exploding in fire. We hear the questions rise
In terrible flame like the whistle of a crazy dog
Like the acid vomit of the fire of Hell
Who and Who and WHO who who
Whoooo and Whooooooooooooooooooooooo!..

The poet was brave indeed and discharged his duties admirably. But from a long-standing poet and no neophyte, one would have expected a subtler, satiric language that would stab at hypocrisy and at the same time disarm. But as that poem stands, its language is too close to that of propaganda. It was this one failure that made him fall out of favour; this near prosaic deployment of a language that should be properly satiric and difficult to arrest.

Professional poets abound today. Are they pimps and prostitutes? Are their poems a form of prostitution? Yes, and yes! Professional poets come in different shapes, but their one sure trademark is that of complicity in their own work, of a pandering to the dictates of the audience—Wordsworth realized this and rejected dictation from the public. He refused to lower his moral standards to meet the poetic fashion of the day as distinct from other poets. Professional poet does nothing else but write poetry, that is, they have no other 'day' job and, are a throwback to the old Roman court poet, always ready to fawn, with an ego only smaller than that of their 'client'— whoever that might be. They are a part of the moral problems in the world, "lending pith to hollow reeds" as Wole Soyinka puts it in a different context concerning certain allegorical characters in *The Interpreters*.

The Poetry in the Pity

A rt is invariably therapeutic, whether so intended or not. The story, poetry, painting, pottery, and most other art forms are ultimately autobiographical in the sense that art derives from lived experience—and a wish to touch, through creativity, some inner core where life springs from, hence the idea of poetry or even ceramics as therapeutic. Lived experience might be traumatic and may lead to psychological conditions capable of unhinging the individual. All art is an outlet for emotional abscess. Of course, here, the emphasis is more on writing.

It is easier and faster to write since the tools needed are, on the one hand, subjective, and, on the other, simple objects like a pen, paper, or almost any rudimentary thing with a scratching tip with which to make marks. This is why prisoners who take to dealing with their experiences automatically choose writing as the form in which to express them. Writing, which some Eurocentric scholars like Popper and Walter Ong have, rightly but exaggeratedly, credited with being the reason for technological advancements, was originally a medium of self-study, introspection, internal dialogue with the psyche, intrinsic meditation, and a form of and for emotional release.

This introspection is a matter of course, since writing is preceded by reading, that is, the reading of our own thoughts before they can take on the permanence of ink or print. As the alphabet displaced orality as a major repository of experience, writing became a more permanent aid to memory according to Walter Ong in "Orality and Literacy"; as such, recourse to writing gives release while, at the same time, recording stages in personal psychic development, and healing processes, which become examples and an aid to the future reader. The equanimity derived from writing is reflected in Roger Chartier's discussion of "the practical impacts of writing"— within an essay of the same title—in the move from the public to the private sphere in England and the USA during the early modern to the modern period. He also insinuates the liberatory power bestowed by writing—through reading.

As an example, it is then understandable that political prisoners from Antonio Gramsci to Wole Soyinka, Jack Mapanje, or Nelson Mandela easily took to writing to empower the self and also to deal with private rumination and the dangers of total mental breakdown. Even career criminals and petty thieves do sometimes take to writing as a process of penance and self-correction and -elevation. Prison is enforced solitude and, in this forced removal from the public sphere, there is a double principle at work: the privacy imposed on the individual by the state and the natural meandering of private thoughts, which leads to introspection and a need to quieten such mental agitations through writing.

Seamus Heaney, in *The Government of the Tongue,* describes such an act of introspection, self-dialogue, and release in the figure of Jesus writing with a stick in the sand while being interpellated by the Pharisees and Sadducees, those eternal aggressive insects, forever biting with their spiteful proboscis. To each of their hostile queries, Jesus Christ described figures in the sand, with a stick, preoccupied by his 'writing' in full meditation before responding. There were subjective mental or inspirational processes at work before he carefully replied to his interlocutors from within an inner inspired resolution.

The individual responds to his or her environment and experiences through writing in differing ways. Ironically, writing as therapy usually achieves its best effect and is most 'inspired' when it is unconscious—as in the case of a non-writer in crisis, who ends up being a writer as a result of those crises—but not when it is contrived and artificial as in so-called 'inspirational poetry,' written as a panacea to all kind of ailments of the mind or weaknesses of character. Moral outrage can be an unconscious well-spring for powerful poetry, as we see in the case of Wilfred Owen. He went to battle practically with a pen in one hand and a gun in the other. The professional necessity of killing further complicates, in this case, the poet's ruminations. The horror of war made a poet out of Owen. In a planned foreword to a future collection, he wrote:

> This book is not about heroes. English Poetry is not
> yet fit to speak of them. Nor is it about deeds, or
> lands, nor anything about glory, honour, might, maj-
> esty, dominion, or power, except war. Above all I am
> not concerned with Poetry. My subject is War, and
> the pity of War. The Poetry is in the pity. Yet these
> elegies are to this generation in no sense consolatory.
> They may be to the next. All a poet can do today is
> warn. That is why true Poets must be truthful.

In other words, his book would contest "The old Lie: Dulce et decorum est /Pro patria mori." Other individuals, the sensitive child, the outsiders and non-conformists, the oppressed, and the ill, become writers through an accidental discovery of the therapeutic activity of writing, while those who are already writers thrive even more from returning to the soothing spaces between words. Enter St. Genet.

Jean Genet's case is a quintessential example of the liberating power of writing. He was born to a prostitute mother, who gave him up for adoption; and progressing through an adoptive home as a child, a penal colony at fifteen, and an infamous stint with the French Foreign Legion from age eighteen, Genet seemed destined for a life of crime and dissolution.

He was a prostitute, petty thief, and vagrant, revolving through the doors of Parisian prisons, where he discovered writing—or writing discovered him—and reached out its therapeutic possibilities. His writings were autobiographies in a literal and literary sense. In Paris he was severally jailed for petty thieving, identity fraud, public indecency, and other offences. The privacy of prison resulted in the poem "Le condamnée mort" and the novel *Our Lady of Flowers* (1944). His life in Europe as a petty thief, homosexual prostitute, and vagabond is recorded in *The Thief's Journal* (1949).

As an adult, even though still in the grip of kleptomania, he rose to become one the foremost French playwrights and leftist activists of the 20th century, who supported the Algerian independence movement, subscribing to Negritude in his play *The Blacks* (1958)—according to Aimé Césaire. His conversion and healing through writing was catalytic after the intervention of leftist Parisian intellectuals like Jean Paul-Sartre, Pablo Picasso, and Jean Cocteau, who, in 1949, saved him from the certain life-sentence of a repeat-offender by petitioning the French president. So promising a literary voice had Genet become.

He went on to help define and shape, with Samuel Becket, what has become 20th century Absurdist Theatre. Although his writings borrow from his dark life, they saved him from the gutters. The darkness that would have enveloped him was transferred unto characters in plays and novels. Genet's life is reminiscent of the words of the character Cecil Graham in Oscar Wilde's *Lady Windermere's Fan*, Act III: "We are all in the gutter, but some of us are looking at the stars."

Oscar Wilde was another tempestuous individual whose writing saved him. In his own words: "God knows; I won't be an Oxford don anyhow. I'll be a poet, a writer, a dramatist. Somehow or other I'll be famous, and if not famous, I'll be notorious. Or perhaps I'll lead the life of pleasure for a time and then—who knows?—rest and do nothing. What does Plato say is the highest end that man can attain here below? To sit down and contemplate the good. Perhaps that will be the end of me too" (Morley, 1976).

Writing delivers the individual from private demons in different ways. It helped William Styron battle depression and the War poets like Siegfried Sassoon live through the daily dismemberment of friends and foes on the battlefield. Poetry has fuelled liberation movements and given succour to the downtrodden. W. H. Auden's quip that poetry makes nothing happen is merely a pessimistic reflection of a poet in a moment of disillusion. Even the ability for him to make that assertion, write it down, and disseminate it in book form is itself an ironic testimony to the liberating act of self-expression. It is a kind of 'talking cure'—in this case the 'writing cure.'

How (Alfred) Noble
is the Nobel Prize?

In a café at the heart of the Latin Quarter in Paris one afternoon in October of 1964, Jean Paul Sartre, that doyen of 20th century French intellectual life, sat down to his usual aperitif when he saw his own face staring back at him from the pages of Le Figaro. The disappointment was so numbing that the drink slipped from grip halfway to his lips. The shattering of glass on polished wooden floor blended with the clash of the jazz drums that were playing in the background. The baguette-munching, tea-sipping clientele moved as one body with the slightest and the politest turn in sympathy with the usually serene head now shaking from side to side in mock shock at the newspaper. Such was the weight he felt that the café itself seemed to turn slightly on its waist with the drag of his body as he read the newspaper. Sartre had just won the Nobel Prize for literature.

That little narration is, of course, inaccurate; events did not proceed in that fashion. But it is a fact that Sartre wrote the Swedish Academy a letter of 'apology' on October 14, 1964, asking himself to be struck out of the list of nominees on which he was rumoured to be numbered. His letter was never read. This was the reason for his fictionalised shock as he sat sipping his bitters or bitterness on the 23rd of the same month. The Nobel committee announced his win on the 24th. Why should this prize have greyed the hair on Sartre's head? The occasion of a Nobel is a moment of joy for many a writer usually. But for the leftist political critic, public intellectual, existentialist philosopher, scourge of Western imperialism, fighter-for-the-oppressed, and a humanist to the bone marrow, this was not the case.

First, it is important to note that Sartre was very anti-establishment in all his writings—novels, plays, scholarly exegesis, or in his political activism. He went beyond the confines of the Ivory Tower to the trenches of 20th century anti-colonial agitation in support of Algeria's FLN and the Negritude Movement and was arrested during the tumultuous Parisian summer of 1968 for 'civil disobedience' in his support of the student revolution strikes. The anti-establishment trajectory of his political engagement and intellectual work was in danger of being 'colonised' by a Western cultural establishment, which he considered a thorough bourgeoisie platform opposed to his socialist beliefs. The reasons ascribed to his being given the award—that his work, in the words of the Nobel judges—is "rich in ideas and filled with the spirit of freedom and the quest for truth [and] has exerted a far-reaching influence on our age" was the same reason, ironically, that Sartre had to reject the prize. He felt that the 'spirit of freedom and the quest for truth' was not served by an institution pitched against those very ideals in the struggle of Western culture against the Eastern—by 'eastern' he clearly meant the 'global south.'

The Sartrean example of moral and political fortitude comes to mind every time the usual general controversies dog a Nobel moment. Concern here is with the politics of the literature prize specifically. Such politics are nevertheless across the board for the science or literature prizes. They have several inflections—the question of whether the award consecrates the right individual in terms of excellence; the problematic of the unduly excluded; and the quarrel about the objectivity or subjectivity of the Swedish Academy's aesthetic valuation in the literature section. More important here as far as literature is concerned, however, is the matter of the ethics, politics, and moral vision of the laureate and, consequently, of the Academy itself as an institutional validator of such politics.

In no other category as in the literature prize is the criticism of the award politics, as reflected in the politics of the consecrated, more resonant. Science is after all a matter of the empiric, even if modes of inhumane research can also raise dust with an observant public. But the ethical and moral questions are more urgent in literature since it is an ideological form, whose modes of representation directly or indirectly impinge upon how people perceive the objective world. The suspect politics of some laureates who have come after Sartre over the years have confirmed his believe that the Swedish Academy is conservative. Two good bad examples are J.M. Coetzee and V.S. Naipaul.

Lucy Valerie Graham says in "Reading the Unspeakable: Rape in J. M. Coetzee's *Disgrace*" that Coatzee, in his critical work and general fictional oeuvre, has always been conscious of, and has engaged with, the question of how rape is (mis)represented and romanticised in classical literature on the one hand, and how it was a tool of racial oppression in colonial, apartheid social (non)interactions on the other. Nevertheless, such knowledge does not amount to much in the one novel, *Disgrace*, where Coetzee engages rape as a political tool in post-apartheid South Africa more directly. The author's narrative fence-sitting has resulted in an international controversy in the popular media and in South Africa's Black political circles over his own moral stand where racial injustice is concerned.

Disgrace is a realistic depiction of post-Apartheid trauma, of which rape is one aspect only besides crime, poverty, HIV, xenophobia—especially against other Black Africans—and White fears of political, economic, and social reprisals. But Coetzee's realism, specifically in the context of rape, is steeped in such elisions, ambivalences, and subtle stereotyping of Black South Africa that it made

Thabo Mbeki remark: "South Africa is not only a place of rape." That remark refers to the central plot of *Disgrace*, which describes the gang rape of a White woman, Lucy, by three Black men on a farm, and the self-confrontation this event produces in her father, who himself is in denial of having raped a Black woman, Melanie—one of his students. The protagonist's father, David Lurie, a university professor, rationalises his having forced himself on a powerless Black female student as a consensual act when asked to speak in his own defence in a disciplinary hearing: "not rape at all, not quite that" he intones, refusing to cooperate.

While the social problem of rape in post-Apartheid South Africa is real, it is nevertheless narrated in such a fashion as to make it the essence of the Black South African male, and indeed of Black humanity. This, against the grain of historical representation of the Black male as a 'phallus symbol' in Frantz Fanon's words, raises questions of moral obligations in any writer when approaching such historically charged topics. Historically, representations of blackness, male or female, in Western travel narratives, colonial documents, or novels have been couched in that and other demonising terms. In a related sense, the history of miscegenation is intimately invested in colonial activity if we consider Ronald Hyam's *Empire and Sexuality*. *Disgrace* occludes this history of the (mis)representation of blackness with a narrative technique, which places the burden of ethical positions and moral filiations with the reader. This is the way Graham justifies the author's ambivalences. But Lynn Higgins and Brenda Silver draw our attention to the novel's masculinist elisions—and, one may add, racial subjectivity—in *Rape and Representation*; elisions such as the silencing of Lucy from talking about her rape directly except in innuendos, or of Melanie's strange quietude about her own abuse in the face of White privilege.

Moreover, Coetzee does not historicise the sexual implica-
tions of the Dutch Empire in South Africa specifically, preferring
to concentrate on effects rather than causes in his narration. Apart
from the sexual subordination of Black bodies—and lands—in the
Western Hemisphere and in different colonial situations, Hyam,
in the particular case of South Africa, asserts that the Dutch East
India Company had a slave lodge at Cape Town. It was a prominent
brothel where slavery, prostitution, and poverty formed a dehuman-
ising blend. The novel would have been more objective had it taken
a historical narrative approach.

The incidence of three random Black men raping a White woman
incorporates all Black men as being complicit in that rape, sim-
plifies the history of race relations in South Africa, and re-enacts
19th century discourses of the 'black peril' which formed the basis
of White fears, draconian apartheid policies, and Black repression.
This can only inspire more antagonism between White and Black
citizens in contemporary South Africa. In the immediacy of White
post-Apartheid anxieties and Black hurt, how does this help to
achieve the peace, progress—not in enlightenment terms—and
harmony that Alfred Nobel envisaged and hoped the Nobel Prizes
would foster? It is instructive that Coetzee, in an interview, did not
see the immediate healing values in Mandela's Truth and Reconciliation Commission, which tried to address a 'history' that he elides
in his prose. Ironically, he leaves it to 'history' to judge the commission's effectiveness, even while he discountenances history in
his own albeit fictional narration. Besides, as the stellar Africanist
critic, Pius Adesanmi, surmised in a private conversation, *Disgrace*,
by its very silence on the topic, carries a subtext which confinesthe
political system of Apartheid and its dehumanisations to the realm
of the 'humanly possible,' and is therefore silent about it. The historical atrocities are simply 'human nature' at work.

Coetzee's political conservatism can be corroborated by the writer's own submissions on his activism or lack thereof in *Doubling the Point,* his collection of essays and interviews. He refers to himself in the third person:

> Politically, the *raznochinets* can go either way. But during his student years he, this person, this subject, my subject, steers clear of the right. As a child in Worcester he has seen enough of the Afrikaner right, enough of its rant, to last him a lifetime. In fact, even before Worcester he has perhaps seen more of cruelty and violence than should have been allowed to a child. So as a student he moves on the fringes of the left without being part of the left. Sympathetic to the human concerns of the left, he is alienated, when the crunch comes, by its language—by all political language, in fact.

It is clear from the above that Coetzee lacks the *littérature engagée,* political activism, and leftist intellection, which preoccupied Sartre particularly, as well as a large percentage of 20th century French leftist intelligentsia more generally such as Andre Breton, Marcel Proust, Andre Gide, Hélène de Beauvoir, Loius Althusser, Merleau-Ponty, Jean-Toussaint Desanti, Dominique Desanti, Jean Kanapa, and many more. It is in representing the humanist ideals of these French leftist intellectuals, artists, writers, and scholars that Sartre had to reject the Nobel Prize. It is not for nothing that Walter Benjamin has described Paris as the cultural capital of the 19th century. Even in its heyday of imperialism, Paris had the saving grace of its humanising left. So stabilising was the force of that left that it ushered in a global democratising transformation by playing metropolitan host to a concentration of liberationist cultural and political movements of the global South that eventually helped to change the course of modern history in the 1960s. Did the conservative politics of a Coetzee need to be institutionalised by the Nobel committee? It is possible to argue that the writer is an individual and has freedom of speech and expression. Even though the Academy has awarded the Nobel to writers who are examples of moral forthrightness in their work such as Wole Soyinka, Doris Lessin, Mario Vargas Llosa, Orhan Pamuk, and others, when the occasional examples of politically conservative winners begin to mount, eyebrows should be raised. Another notable conservative is V.S. Naipaul.

Naipaul's brand of racial discourse in his novels, specifically his demonization of people of colour, is well known and has been much commented upon to be worth elaboration here. No less a critic than Edward Said—whose 1978 seminal work on misrepresentation, *Orientalism*, launched postcolonial criticism in the Western academy—says of Naipaul in *Said on Naipaul* that the latter has "allowed himself quite consciously to be turned into a witness for the Western prosecution" thereby encouraging "colonial mythologies about wogs and darkies." That should be enough said about Naipaul's conservatism and his perennial demonization of the Third World, which others have ascribed to a twisted psychology of self-hate. But there is need to recall Derek Walcott as witness, if only because, like Naipaul, he is from the Caribbean. A little anecdote will suffice. The New Statesman reports Walcott famously opening a Calabash Literary Festival reading in Jamaica in 2008 with the warning: "I'm going to be nasty." He proceeded to satirise Naipaul in verse with the poem, "The Mongoose," which opens with the lines: "I have been bitten. I must avoid infection. Or else I'll be as dead as Naipaul's fiction." Rather simple and straightforward from the poet who gave us the Nobel-winning epic *Omeros*. Perhaps Walcott simply needed to deliver a direct metaphoric punch to Naipaul's conservative proboscis. The darkness, and racism of most of Naipaul's oeuvre, is captured more evocatively in another Walcott poem, where he refers to the former as "V.S. Nightfall."

Why is it that, every so often, the Nobel committee chooses for their laureate a writer whose work is indirectly likely to lead to or has led to divisionary politics on the border of hate speech? Predictably, such writers are usually those for whom literature, according to Sartre, is a bourgeoisie preoccupation as opposed to real-life political activism or even critical and progressive textual engagement. It is instructive that the Nobel committee, in awarding Naipaul the 2001 Literature prize, remarked in their citation that: "Naipaul is Conrad's heir as the annalist of the destinies of empires in the moral sense: what they do to human beings. His authority as a narrator is grounded in the memory of what others have forgotten, the history of the vanquished."

Such a citation is nothing more than an unwitting indictment of Naipaul, the writer, for his dark and demonising visions and denigration of subject peoples in the same vein as Joseph Conrad, particularly in *The Heart of Darkness*; Africa, on the one hand, and the global South, on the other, being those 'areas of darkness'—to echo the title of another of Naipaul's sad works. Conrad's *Heart of Darkness* has been severally deconstructed by postcolonial critics as being covertly prejudicial, or downright racist in Chinua Achebe's summation, which has led to a re-reading of Conrad and his revaluation in the British canon.

As far as Naipaul is concerned, besides the literary, several biographers (official and unofficial)—amongst them Henry Theroux and Patrick French—have recounted the sexual sadism and demonic personality of Naipaul. While it can be argued that the Nobel committee may not look at a writer's life but at the life of his work, to what extent does this psychotic personality transfer into his demonization of cultures? How does this warp his vision as a writer? Naipaul is a man so insensitive that no sooner was his wife of 41 years in a fresh-dug grave than he remarried—in two months flat; moreover, the same wife had been sent to an early grave due to his philandering with concubines, mistresses, and prostitutes, all of whom he subjected to sexual violence. How noble then is the Nobel if the writer's right-wing politics and his psychotic personality are irrelevant in the administration of the award?

Escapist arguments will have it that we should separate the life of a writer from the lives of his work, as suggested earlier. Most importantly, the grey area of poetic license and an undifferentiated freedom of expression will be marshalled as talking points— particularly since the novel is simply 'art.' Nevertheless, 'art for art's sake' is precisely the kind of bourgeoisie irritation which 20th century French intellection eschewed. left to the Nobel committee, we will be trapped in the 20th century still in political terms. The writer is still the conscience of society, "the unacknowledged legislators of the world" in Percy Shelley's formulation in the 1821 essay, "In Defence of Poesie." It seems to be clear that the Swedish Academy automatically lionises those writers like Naipaul, Coetzee, or Rudyard Kipling, whose Eurocentrism is either apparent or very obvious and whose politics support the status quo in the world in contradiction of the progressive political goals for which Alfred Nobel endowed and willed money to prizes in science and literature.

The Eurocentrism and status quo mentality of Western literary and prize awards institutions are exemplified in a strange but perfectly market-logical 1950 request by Alfred Kopf Publishers that Doris Lessing, 2007 Nobel Laureate, edit the manuscript of *The Grass is Singing*. According to Lucy Valerie Graham and in the South African terms of the discourse of the black peril:

Doris Lessing's New York publisher, Alfred Knopf,
told Lessing they would consider *The Grass is Singing*
for publication if she would change it to accommodate
an explicit rape of the White female protagonist by
Moses, a Black man: "in accordance," as the publishers put it, "with the mores of the country" [South
Africa]. Lessing refused the attempted revision, claim-
ing: "the whole point of *The Grass is Singing* was the
unspoken devious codes of behavior of the Whites."
When the novel came out in paperback, the writer was
shocked to find on its front cover "a lurid picture of
a blond cowering terrified while a big buck nigger ...
stood over her, threatening her with a panga." In the
minds of publishers at least, such 'porno-tropics' evi-
dently made for lucrative publications.

The Nobel committee now and again seems to partake of the
kind of stereotypical aesthetic valuation described by Graham—
but for a different reason. The publisher is thinking of monetising
fictionalised lived experience while the Swedish academy, it will
seem, is invested in keeping the power relations in the world as it
is—hardly ever is there a situation where there is not something to
be gained ideologically by the West as represented by this Academy.

An example was the 2010 Nobel Peace Prize award to the Chinese dissident, Liu Xiaobo, who sits in a Chinese jail and could not
physically travel to Europe or be represented even by his wife, who
is under surveillance. Under the pretence of patronage, Stockholm
morally aligned itself with the USA and EU in a struggle for economic and political supremacy between the West and a waking red
giant. The Academy's action was cleverly subsumed under the discourse of freedom of speech and democracy; those two most abused

and exploited panaceas for assumed human rights infringements in the global South—even when those same human rights abuses are rampant in a racist Europe which still haunts, maims, and kills the innocent on its streets due to colour or other imagined 'infirmities.' It is this kind of dissimulation and duplicity that Alfred Nobel wanted to assuage with the progressive agenda of the Nobel prizes; but the Academy has learnt nothing from the lessons of history since it promotes conservative and politically dangerous art. Graham's tongue in cheek support of *Disgrace* also derives from this kind of conservative politics because, after recalling the example of efforts to corrupt Lessing and her refusal to be an establishment prop Graham still writes:

> While the commercial success of Coetzee's latest novel may be attributed to similar international appetites, it is possible to argue that in *Disgrace* Coetzee self-consciously performs a subversion of 'black peril' narrative—by simultaneously scripting what Sol T. Plaatje referred to as 'the White peril,' the hidden sexual exploitation of black women by White men that has existed for centuries.

A deconstruction of Graham's analyses will show clearly that Coetzee invokes 'White peril' only in a tokenist manner; the better to enlarge his demonization of the Black characters in his novel on the one hand and promote a conservative politics of the status quo on the other. History is the fault of the Black South African in multiracial South Africa, he seems to say. The Nobel committee rather agrees with him and hands him a laureateship. But conscience is a very disturbing genie; it is little wonder Coetzee had to flee South Africa to live in Australia.

The Nobel committee ought to realize that literature is not a tea party; it can liberate or imprison the spirit. Even Charles de Gaulle, intemperate imperialist, had to bow before the liberating power of writing. He had no choice but to order the immediate and unconditional release of Jean Paul Sartre, who was arrested and detained during the student strikes in the summer of 1968. In decreeing Sartre's release, de Gaulle became philosophical: "You don't arrest Voltaire." About time the Nobel committee realize: 'you don't arrest the human spirit.'

Tax and Syn/tax

First, dividing the word 'syntax' into its constituent syllables is not merely for stylistic flourish nor is it just a scribal genuflection to a postmodern quirk. One rather wishes to coerce some cumulative synthesis of meaning from the possible accidence in the root 'syn' and the 'accident' in the morpheme and suffix 'Tax' and 'tax,' respectively, in their relative proximity, all within an overarching semantic field while discussing how a sentence or line is, or should be, constructed in poetry.

To consider the semantic accretions possible in 'syn/tax,' one could begin to think of the root syn- in some multiplicity of ways to help exemplify, but not necessarily prescribe, what a healthy piece of poem should look like. 'Syntax,' of course, is naturally visible in 'syn/tax,' and this implies each sentence construction within the poem in relation to each other, to the whole poem, and as a unit—word order, in short. Someone described "finding the right syntax for a poem" as being "like finding the right light before you take a photograph." The idea of a photograph is important, as we shall see. Furthermore, the syntax of poetry should not be like the syntax of prose, as is now more and more the contemporary poetic 'habit'—which needs curbing. We could also consider the synchronic as juxtaposed against the diachronic in syntactic poetic construction. In that light, one needs to look at what the history of syntactical practices was like (i.e., its diachrony) and what is it like today (i.e., its synchrony). This brings us to a consideration of the question of traditional and modern predilections.

Traditional English poetry explored the full range of English prosody, metre, and rhyme in all its variation, sometimes stilted—especially in the light of the changes that have overtaken language and expression with the onset of time: hence the natural arrival of the modernist impulse, which moves closer to the tonalities of contemporary speech and shuns what has become, in diction and syntax, an archaism of the distant past. One would not expect to read a poem beginning 'thou' today, certainly, nor a line carrying the whole fusillade of traditional prosody. Sometimes, though, there is a marrying of tradition and modernity. So, we could have a modernist free verse in 21st century diction but garlanded with the heroic couplet of the restoration period (as practiced by, for example, Dryden in Absalom and Achitophel or Macflecknoe) or with the rhyme scheme of a Shakespearian sonnet from the Elizabethan period. Some contemporary poets still retain past forms, such as the sonnet, today.

After historical upheavals like colonialism and decolonisation and the contemporary postcolonial moment, the equation has become more complex. We have postcolonial poets from the former English colonies who have inherited the linguistics burden of English and work in that language. Traumatic enough as that history is, the reality is that the postcolonial poet who dips richly into English and his or her own native literary store—be it written or oral—is very rich indeed in the range of the sources and examples to borrow from. Oral literature in Africa for example, not to talk of India—with its ancient Vedic tradition—has the verbal equivalencies of what we call prosody within poetry in English, and other poetic conceits. As such, the postcolonial is richer in his or her hybridity. Of course, it is not a simple, problem-free hybridity, but this is not a place to delve into the cultural politics of acquired language.

The extents to which such postcolonial poets scour the archives of native and English traditions are varied, depending on the poet.

Usually, linguistic appropriation results in the use of English diction with the tonality of the native tongue overlaid upon it to a greater or lesser degree and to multifarious rhythmical effects, depending on which poet is in question. We have examples in the earlier work of Derek Walcott up till *Omeros*, in Niyi Osundare's homespun tonal ranges or Tanure Ojaide's ululating Urhobo accent, in Pius Adesanmi's incantatory chant in *The Wayfarer and other Poems*. There are those African poets like Christopher Okigbo and Wole Soyinka whose tonalities are more steeped in the rhythms of classical English prosody, although shorn of its usual cumbersome metre; that is, they are modernist in the usual sense of the word. The moral, as insinuated in T.S. Eliot's essay "Tradition and the Individual Talent," is that the 'individual poet' has to find a metrical and syntactical—even lyrical—niche compatible with, and useful to, his or her own talents within the provisions of tradition and then progress from there. The reluctance to look back upon tradition is where the contemporary avant-garde stumbles. The 'newness' that it seeks to propose is not real and suffers from a refusal to borrow enough as prop before discarding the scaffoldings of tradition. According to Eliot:

> One of the facts that might come to light in this
> process is our tendency to insist, when we praise
> a poet, upon those aspects of his work in which he
> least resembles anyone else. In these aspects or parts
> of his work we pretend to find what is individual,
> what is the peculiar essence of the man. We dwell
> with satisfaction upon the poet's difference from his
> predecessors, especially his immediate predecessors;
> we endeavour to find something that can be isolated
> in order to be enjoyed. Whereas if we approach a
> poet without this prejudice we shall often find that

> not only the best, but the most individual parts of
> his work may be those in which the dead poets, his
> ancestors, assert their immortality most vigorously.
> And I do not mean the impressionable period of ado-
> lescence, but the period of full maturity.

This approximation of rhythm and syntax in verse is not idle but ultimately closely related to each other. And thus, we come to 'synaesthesia'—sensory images empowered by diction and these, in turn, inform rhythm and syntax or vice-versa. Sensory images are inherent in words appealing to the senses of sight, touch, taste, smell, hearing, feeling of action, and of general sense impression. Diction that has more of such evocative appeals, and which are arranged in the 'right order,' help to achieve the aforementioned 'lighting'—that is, the right syntax—needed to 'photograph' the healthy poem. A keen ear or a good musical sense aids in arranging evocative diction to arrive at the right metre—even though it is that of free verse—and thus the right syntax. Of course, 'wit' or the 'defamiliarised' expression should be interwoven into syntax. Here is one from Eliot and Okigbo respectively, both fine modernist poets: "I will show you fear in a fistful of dust" and "how does one say No in thunder…" The first quote is from Eliot's *The Wastelands* and the second from Okigbo's "Silences 1: Lament of the Silent Sisters" in *Collected Poems*. The best way to learn to do this is to read other poets who have done it successfully (is it Dryden who opines that "Imitation is the spur of wit"?) from the ancients to the moderns: Dryden, Pope, Hopkins, Eliot, Coleridge, Walcott, Okigbo, Soyinka, Tati-Loutard, and uncountable others. In short, the poet's recourse can only be to tradition.

Bad lighting or opaque diction does not, naturally, improve syntax since it is bound to remove something from wit, probably restrict the field of signification, and distort overall musicality. The idea is that the poet should strive for "a fine balance," which allows for an appeal to the rhythm of contemporary speech without sounding pedestrian, while simultaneously achieving syntactical grace and avoiding a feeling in the reader of the contrived. To take an example, here is Olu Oguibe in his collection, *A Gathering Fear*: "I am bound to this land by blood/That is why my vision is blurred/I am rooted in its soil/ And its streams flood my veins..."! It is simple, everyday diction, strengthened in its emotional reach through its imagistic appeal as in 'bound' (i.e., being tied and constrained, imprisoned) and in the metaphorical resonance of the same 'bound' heightened by the alliteration and assonance in 'blood,' 'blurred,' and 'flood.' The lexical displacement of 'blood' for streams in "and its streams flood my veins" is powerfully effective as 'and its blood flood my veins' will never ever be! Besides, the word stream, read through the lenses of M. Freeman's cognitive linguistics and prototypical semantics (1997:4) as refracted through Belekova's "Cognitive Models of Verbal Poetic Images," immediately and clearly suggests to the reader, in its archetypical coding, that the poet is in a big city and misses a small town or village; it is a cry from the metropolis to the town; "a song from exile." The "poetic image space" of the work is very evocative and moves under a lyrical tug that is the syntactical construction, fusing sound and sense, wit and meter. That is a poet working in true modernist mode, borrowing from tradition and finding his own individual voice in a very resonant manner. Image and diction mesh with rhythm and syntax in the utterance to arrive at meaning and poignancy.

This example shows how important image/diction is to rhythm/ syntax and wit/sense. A further reading of the poem simply confirms and emphasises this probing. There are numerous examples of powerful poetry like this one, but sadly, there are also even more numerous examples of bad poems out there, chief of which are the so-called prose poems, slam poetry, dub poetry, sound poetry, and so on. They coalesce within the ambience of the contemporary avant-garde. Of course, such forms of counterculture are useful and necessary but fall short of what one would refer to as poetry, whatever other form of art they might be called. Luckily, there is still good poetry for the careful seeker: the temptation is strong not to exclude examples such as "the night is dark/the waters are deep/and the lost child flounders/between the dark and the deep" from Harry Garuba's "Fragments" in the BBC anthology *The Fate of Vulture*. Another example is Chiedu Ezeanah's lines "Go to water, go rivering/where the eye that looks becomes a brook" from "Song of the Musician of Waters" in *The Twilight Trilogy*.

It is not a clear-cut matter to decide when the syntax overshoots the mark or stays within or behind the limits of proportion. The result is usually immediately apparent, though—especially when the poem is read out loud or in contemplation. It is remarkable that, mostly these days, a poet, in straining for the cadence of common speech within a syntax that is—at the same time—poetic, vacillates between sheer prose and contrived inversion or versified or rhymed prose, opaque diction, and sometimes bombast—disguised, perhaps, as a sentimental unrestrained political harangue. One good bad example is "Someone Bombed America" by Amiri Baraka.

The matter of opacity as it subtracts from a healthy poetic syntax steeped in the rhythm of everyday speech is important because there is, indeed, a symbiotic relationship between diction, rhythm, and syntax, with the last being the framework around which the previous two cohere; all improve or diminish each other. That is, of course, debatable because it is easy to argue that all items are so inter-meshed that there is a simultaneous chemical reaction taking place at the creative moment. So closely allied to each other are diction, rhythm, and syntax that opaque diction excludes the reader or hearer's senses, killing the light in the 'photograph' of the poem—such that the impact on the emotional and spiritual or subliminal level is absent. There is no resonance but dead words, dead since language is supposed to be a breathing, living thing. But that kind of language would not speak to us.

If diction is opaque, it does not allow for the central engine of modernist rhythm—imagism coupled with a healthy syntax; it does not help in achieving the necessary target of a natural cadence nor does it improve syntax. There is the anecdote of the king who demanded an original and everlasting wise saying from a passing sage. The king was replied to with: "...and this too shall pass away." The word order makes that sentence, in and of itself, poetic, aided by its anti-climactic rhythm and its sense of finality, of ineluctable decline and ruin; its ironic humanising slap at the regal figure of king and kingdom... "And this too shall pass away." If we were to change the syntax and write instead 'and this shall pass away too,' there is an immediate jarring note and a departure from the careful lilting solemnity of rhythm, resulting in the run-of-the mill. 'And this shall pass away too' becomes pedestrian without being poetic while 'and this too shall pass away' is poetic while avoiding to seem contrived, irrespective of the use of the slightly formal 'shall.' Actually, 'shall' serves for a poeticising gambit in the sentence. 'And this too will pass away,' would fall short woefully. Even though that originary sentence is in isolation of any other line and not part of the full body of a poem, it nevertheless sets an emotional wave in motion, whose concentric arcs the hearer or reader imaginatively begins to fill out with the absent 'body' of a full poem. This is helped along by the image, a sensing of something 'passing' away. The hearer or reader is in the grip of a poem that is obviously not written out. This is what effective syntax should do: expand the field of signification to emotionally include the unspoken. That sentence is also brief. Shakespeare contends that "brevity is the soul of wit," and so it is! We hear brevity, wit, and emotional and spiritual resonance in that tiny creative moment. The reader can imagine that the sage walked on lugubriously while the king stared after him in awe and bewilderment, humbled.

And now the idea of tax! In most modern democracies we all pay tax on our yearly earnings towards the smooth running of state and public facilities, such as roads. This is one way to view the idea of taxation as it relates to poetry; that is, tax as a giving up of our excess lexicographic earnings within one dictionary-year; consider the dictionary as being equivalent to a constant 'year' in the work-life of a poet. Another way of seeing it would be to consider taxation in a symbolic sense and ascribe to it, for our purpose, all situations where the individual has to discipline the self, give things or habits, like smoking, up. Such self-deprivations can be equated to fasting for the general well-being of the organism (the organism in this case being poetry); what has become known in chic circles as detoxication or 'detox'.

Another similar analogy between tax and poetry can be that of curbing over-indulgence, which, again, would be close to fasting—in the sense of eating only what is necessary; sweets, snacks, and other munchies being jettisoned just as the common dessert would be. In other words, nothing but a well-balanced, sufficient but non-superfluous repast should be the goal; especially so for the poet who, like a priest with higher callings, should be a frugal eater and not gluttonous. It is sensible eating in short, prevention being proverbially better than cure. It would be difficult to break a habit of long-winded syntactical constructions, accruing from word-drunkenness. No amount of exercise would ever deflate a mountain of belly with already fixed digestive borders! The same is true with poetic eating habits—words being the food items in the poetic belly and the sentence or line being the whole meal in combination, and a judicious and sparing use of words being a way of assuring a lean, healthy poem throughout its life. As such, the poet must eat words sensibly—not overindulge himself or herself; that is, use words sensibly, not overuse them; otherwise, the poem becomes fat or obese.

Finally, in 'syntagma' we will merge all the trains of thought so far. The paradigmatic axis of poetic composition is the poem itself and the syntagmatic axis is the words as they occur in the line or syntax. The syntax is enhanced by the diction and the image that they resonate together. Should there be faults in the syntagmatic axis, the paradigm itself becomes fractured. Diction is important in relation to each other within the poem as their cumulativeness results in either an effective, natural, or defective rhythm, which then takes away from the overall impact of the poem, supposedly propelled forward or held back as much as the images aid in expanding or contracting the field of signification. Choice of words becomes important, and the poet's lexicon must allow for such a lexical variation as could enable the right combination of the right words. A guide is that, usually, if a word can be replaced in a line with the rhythm and sense remaining much the same, then the right word was not chosen in the first place. It should be difficult or impossible to replace a word in a line of verse. As for wit and a uniqueness of expression, brevity, according to Shakespeare, should be a guiding principle. So, all those prose poems out there are mostly fat and overweight; besides, certain syntactic constructions are also archaic or trite and tired in modern poetry. One such is the prepositional phrase (i.e., the noun + of + noun): the mother of all battles, the river of life etc. even if, sometimes, they function well if deployed sparingly in the hands of a very experienced poet. It is much better to avoid them. They are very lazy craft-worn constructions. Sometimes language insinuates itself to the poet, who becomes word-drunk and falls into a vomit of words, unrestrained and undisciplined. For the careful poet, the guide should be tradition. In the words of Eliot once more:

> Tradition is a matter of much wider significance.
> It cannot be inherited, and if you want it, you must
> obtain it by great labour. It involves, in the first place,
> the historical sense, which we may call nearly indis-
> pensable to anyone who would continue to be a poet
> beyond his twenty-fifth year; and the historical sense
> involves a perception, not only of the pastness of the
> past, but of its presence; the historical sense compels
> a man to write not merely with his own generation
> in his bones, but with a feeling that the whole of
> the literature of Europe from Homer and within it
> the whole of the literature of his own country has a
> simultaneous existence and composes a simultaneous
> order.

A word is enough for the poet!

Acknowledgement

These essays first appeared in the *Maple Tree Literary Supplement* (MTLS) literary journal in slightly different forms as editorials for specific editions of the Ezine. The essay, "The Example of Mandela" is anthologized as "The Peaceful "Trouble!" in *Mandela: Tributes to a Global Icon* (Falola 2014).

About the Book

Imagination's Many Rooms is a well-crafted collection of bristling essays on different but related subjects. Partly socio-political and literary commentary, partly a young poet's reminiscences and encounters with global literary and cultural icons, the individual pieces are thematically grouped into sections in an organic anthology. It is written in a highly arresting style, with two of the pieces being essayistic conversations with a dead Canadian writer and a dead Nigerian scholar-poet respectively.